Architecture in a Crowded World

By the same author

Architecture in a Crowded World

Vision and Reality in Planning

Lionel Brett

SCHOCKEN BOOKS • NEW YORK

First SCHOCKEN edition 1971

For Christiana with love

Contents

Foreword

'The art of writing,' said Logan Pearsall Smith, 'is the art of making people real to themselves with words.' My first object has been to attempt this for the generally non-introspective architect. In so doing I hope to achieve my second, which is to expose the mind of the architect to other people. But I think we are almost at the end of a culture in which this was possible because professionals and laymen spoke the same language. If we are, this may be the last book to make the attempt. Even now, I know that it will be too simple for some architects and too complicated for some laymen. For we are approaching a situation in which even literate and concerned people are not going to understand the language in which planning and architecture are discussed. I certainly find the minds, or anyhow the words, of some of our most serious writers on architecture depressingly opaque. Where in my case clarity and depth have come into conflict, natural limitations have I hope settled the issue in favour of the former.

Writers who have most influenced me have been, in order of discovery, Le Corbusier, Ruskin, Geddes and his great follower Mumford, Lilienthal, Banham and Venturi. Hence the anthological character of parts of the book; for all we are is what a thousand predecessors have made us.

I would like to thank the Librarian of the Royal Institute of British Architects and his staff for their ungrudging assistance.

I

Parameters

Most of us spend our lives in a totally man-made environment, which we totally repudiate. Indians on their hopeless mud-plains, Americans in their sedans, Englishwomen in their precincts, teeming Italians in their beautiful slums, endure an anti-human environment as fatalistically as a bad climate. We know we made it, as we know we make wars at intervals, but we feel equally powerless to do anything about either compulsion. The index of wealth is not in our collective power to change it, but in our individual power to escape from it. The richest entirely do, the poorest never will, and the rest manage something between a fortnight at the seaside and a week-end cottage in the country – merrily making matters worse in the process.

It is not hard to see the reasons for this sense that our environment is unsatisfying but that there is nothing to be done about it. The physical shape of things – the totality of towns and country – was just about the last thing to be brought under social control. Until our own day, the townscapes and landscapes of Europe were either as unwilled as those of Africa – the resultant of innumerable individual forces each pulling their own way – or they were laid out by some prince or other high contracting party miles above the heads of ordinary people. Local self-government was a matter of adjusting rival claims and making life as bearable as possible within a frame of reference utterly given.

This was understandable and acceptable because for a couple of thousand years no new techniques arrived to disturb traditional patterns of living. The changes that occurred were in men themselves and in what went on inside them. When finally in nineteenth-century England the built environment suddenly did become intolerable, human nature adapted itself as stoically as to a war or an earthquake. Great works of art flowered on the dunghill. Conversely, the garden cities and other model communities appeared to be the negation of art, and it seemed inconceivable that any Dickens or Baudelaire would see the light of day in a New Town.

Art flowered, and roots clung. Before long, the home-making instinct had attached itself as fondly and as blindly to the world's slums as to any war-time dugout or seaman's hammock. They had to be cleared by force. Workers and intellectuals, equally alienated, became dependent on alienation as a stimulant and took an equal dislike to do-gooders who planned to deprive them of it.

Yet it is absolutely out of the question for us to be content with this state of affairs. The technological and economic and political forces that generate change are nowadays infinitely more powerful than the inertia that resists it, and there is no escape from the age-old and not necessarily losing battle to change for the better. The unique thing about our age is that with all the weaponry to hand we find this battle so hard to win. To understand why this is so is the first step to a break-out, and this we can only do by taking the whole process to pieces and putting it together again so that its workings are clear to us. This is the aim of the chapters that follow.

Buildings have three uses: *functional* – they shelter our activities; *environmental* – they create the scene on which we act out our lives; and *symbolic* – they represent to us larger than life certain ideas current in our societies at the time they are built. The people who create them are human beings, part rational, part intuitive. So first we look at the simple external forces or parameters that act upon our built environment and start the moulding process which more complex inner forces carry to what passes for completion.

2

This is unquestionably where it all begins – with the primeval dilemma. What Eve needed was the garden of Eden; what she wanted was a certain apple. Architects know where they stand here – shoulder to shoulder with Karl Marx. 'It is the artist's privilege,' they have been taught, 'to give the public what it doesn't know it wants.' All the accusations of arrogance derive from this claim. Let us examine its validity.

Wants manifestly have their dark side. They can be ignorant, selfish, mutually exclusive. According to all the moralities, they are easier satisfied than needs, only to turn to dust and ashes. Because they are by definition wholly self-regarding, they may be anti-social, and because they are instinctive they are often incompatible with one another.

Yet their language is the only one in which people can express, for themselves, their needs. Unless this language is attended to, we shall find ourselves using indirect substitutes, such as political theory or mere hunches, with all their liabilities to error or self-deception. In his great lecture *Two Concepts of Liberty*, Sir Isaiah Berlin is concerned with the dangers of what Kant called the greatest despot imaginable – paternalism.

This is the argument used by every dictator, inquisitor, and bully, who seeks some moral, or even aesthetic, justification for his conduct. I must do for men (or with them) what they cannot do for themselves, and I cannot ask their permission or consent, because they are in no condition to know what is best for them. . . . I may declare that they are actually aiming at what in their benighted state they consciously resist, because there exists within them an occult entity – their latent rational will, or their 'true' purpose – and that this entity, although it is belied by all that they overtly feel and do and say, is their 'real' self, of which the poor empirical self in space and time may know nothing or little; and that this inner spirit is the only self that deserves to have its wishes taken into account.

Since these words were spoken in 1958 the Rule of Experts against which they were directed has marched on. Government

3

has become more complex and esoteric, economics more incomprehensible and mass opinion more cynical and unreliable. Now the danger signals are hoisted and there is much talk of curing these evils by increased public participation. We have seen speculators placing their projects on public exhibition, with all the P.R. stops pulled out, in an appeal to the masses against expert opinion.

So the simple proposition that buildings are shaped by human needs is less simple than it sounds. Who is to be their spokesman, the building's users, the people (generally different) who pay for it, the sociologists who study our present society, the planners who are supposed to project its future, the citizens who are going to have to look at it, or the architect with his analysis and his synthesis? The answer is, of course, all; and since somebody has to collate all these needs and wants and projections and embrace them in the built form, this will generally be the architect, on the principle that questions are best asked by the man who will be held responsible for the answers. It should now be clear that he will be concerned with much more than somebody's expressed wants or his own hunch about their true needs. Time and space, past present and future, are the unseen forces that in a living community will speak through the voices of planners, preservationists, owners, neighbours, investors and politicians. If they are unrepresented in the final synthesis that shapes the building, it will be in trouble from them later on.

Climate, site and scene

Because we are altering the face of the world, one inescapable parameter is the piece of earth and air we intend to occupy. Weather and situation must affect the building's form functionally and the local scene aesthetically – or so you would think. But historically this has by no means always been so nor have architectural writers, with the honourable exception of Vitruvius, even remembered to say it ought to be. The Parthenon has been reproduced on the banks of the Danube, there are Palladian palaces

4

in Bengal and Leningrad, Gothic cathedrals in the tropics and Moghul domes in the Cotswolds. On the whole, the grander the building the less regard it paid to geo-physical facts: the cottages faced the sun, but the squire beneath his portico lived in perpetual shadow – a victim of his architect's, and maybe his own, fashionable sense of priorities, calling

> The winds through long arcades to roar,
> Proud to catch cold at a Venetian door*

The reasons for this state of affairs are clear. Primitive building, like primitive cooking, could not afford to disguise its raw materials or to go far afield for them. It was an organic part of its native earth or forest, for it was nothing more than a minor rearrangement of their materials.

Sophisticated building, like sophisticated cooking, was at pains to use exotic ingredients or at least to disguise its more homely ones. Primitive building, again, had to adapt itself to the terrain, and in doing so produced the subterranean houses of North China, the cliff-hanging houses of Sicily and Spain, the reed houses of the Euphrates delta, the tree and lake houses of New Guinea and Ceylon, the skyscrapers of the Yemen – architecture more ingenious and exotic than anything the professionals have dreamed of. These strange results arose not from fancy, but from facts – the elementary facts of geo-physics.

First, climate. Countries with cold winters will turn the faces of buildings to the sun and glaze them, but will warmly wrap their backs. If their summers are hot, these glazed fronts will be shuttered or louvred or arcaded, making a powerful pattern of shadows. Wet climates will shape their roofs to channel the downpours easily away, and will throw a shelter of some sort over every footway. Humid countries will slide walls away to invite the wind, dry or cold countries will seal everything to shut it out and streamline shapes to deflect it so it makes less noise. Dull climates will cultivate the sky, brilliant climates the shade. Microclimate even, the difference between one corner of a field and another,

* Alexander Pope, *Epistle to Lord Burlington* (1731).

will shape buildings, and when they huddle together each will seize any tiny privilege of view or sun it can, like a street crowd watching a procession.

Of course some environments are so hostile – through intense heat or cold or dirt or noise – that buildings will have no alternative but to isolate themselves entirely by air conditioning, artificial lighting and sound insulation. In those circumstances climate loses its shape-making properties, and pure form, cradled like a womb in a net of services, will emerge from the quite different influences we shall be considering in later chapters. The aircraft and space-ship are mobile examples of the same condition, though the latter is still at the primitive phase of being a pure environmental mechanism or machine for living in.

Then sites. The word 'climate' derives from the Greek word for a slope. Slopes facing the equator feel inviting; slopes facing the poles repel. So from the sea the coastline of the Riviera is a mass of faces, but from inland the audience is as inconspicuous as in a well-raked theatre. In the northern landscape, warm sheltered corners will be seized or created, in the south one will perch on the cool edges of hills. Buildings will settle into spaces like an animal in a thicket, completing the picture. Windows like eyes will make landscapes out of nothing by throwing a frame round them, doors create vistas simply through being walked through. So the inter-action between the inner and the outer world which is the essence of architecture starts at this ordinary physical level.

Most often, there is more to it than this. New buildings join an older group, or even have to take their place in a vast concourse. Then new problems arise, new also in the sense that only in this century have people bothered their heads with them. True, Wren and Hawksmoor took the trouble to go Gothic in appropriate surroundings, and until the Gothic Revival it was considered only decent to complete a classical composition in the appropriate or even identical language. But these exceptional instances were no part of the theory of architecture and were not mentioned in the textbooks, which assumed virgin sites and applied themselves to fundamentals. 'Good manners' in architecture, as something gener-

6

ally to be preferred to originality, was a characteristically English invention of the 1920s and 30s. It was part of the last-ditch defence of our heritage against modernism associated with Germans and Jews, and as a symptom of that heritage's loss of vitality and relevance it was deeply suspect to the younger generation.

The dust of those aesthetic battles of Britain has long settled and we now live in a duller and more consensus-minded age. Now the dogma is that new buildings should have regard not to the style but to the scale, texture and colour of their neighbours, and great numbers of them have that and nothing more, as becomes absurdly apparent when the neighbours are removed. This is well-trodden territory tirelessly patrolled by planning officers and best explored by doing rather than by writing, but this much is worth remembering. There is a law of entropy ceaselessly at work in the man-made world, by which everything tends, if left to itself, towards uniformity. The cause is simply that people learn from one another. The process was held back for centuries by poor communications, primitive technology and the need to make do with local resources. Even so it steadily persisted. Now all these impediments are swept away and the differences between places become more precious as they become more precarious. Anything the designer can do, even to the point of affectation, to keep them alive will make the world more interesting to live in.

Economics

Another word for these external parameters is constraints, and at this point this word may be thought more appropriate. But it is to be avoided, even here, since it suggests something cramping and negative, whereas the way to look at all parameters, financial and other, is as helping hands towards the realisation of significant form in what would otherwise be a formless universe.

We do not really think of economics as affecting architecture

7

until the nineteenth century. Of course through all history the rich used building as a form of display, the poor got themselves housed as best they could within severe economic constraints, and the moderately prosperous had to think twice before climbing from the stucco bracket into the stone one. But by and large the shacks of the poor have reverted to topsoil and all that remains of the cities of the past are bourgeois houses and monuments, few of which, like the Tuscan churches that never achieved their marble fronts, show signs of economic strain. The rich might grumble but they paid up.

Building at minimum cost can be done in two ways. The first is mass production using standard components or standard houses. It was the population explosion which first gave the mass production of buildings an impetus and then an aesthetic of its own. Both developed initially in England, whose sea defences permitted her cities to sprawl without walls and her artisans to live down on the ground in terrace houses each with its own front door. Elsewhere, from the earliest days of imperial Rome, cities were forced by their constricting walls upwards rather than outwards, and urban populations were housed in multi-storey constructions in which it would not have occurred to anyone to give the individual dwelling any outward expression. Consequently the rhythm that we get from serial repetition never materialised.

The London terrace house of the eighteenth century was the first example of what is now called 'rat-trad' construction. It was designed and built by small craftsmen with the aid of pattern books that began to appear in the 1720s; its components were kits of parts as standardised as anything churned out by modern die-presses. But because they were cut from natural materials nobody except a few Victorian visionaries have ever complained of their monotony. To most non-technical people they still make the case for simple serial repetition of dwellings both practically and aesthetically, and they were often called to witness by functionalists of the older generation in the campaign to kill sentimentality and the one-off dream house and get back to 'the House Machine, the mass-production home, healthy (and morally so too) and beautiful

8

in the same way that the working tools which accompany our existence are beautiful'.

Like most morally healthy propositions, Le Corbusier's has not caught on. Working for the most part in dehumanised anonymous environments people want their homes to represent the opposite pole. Life in the filing cabinet is repudiated in those countries where people are allowed to express an opinion. Even the English terrace house, the most civilised kind of urban living yet invented, is condemned not for itself but for its Victorian working-class associations, and can only be sold to two groups: those who cannot afford anything better and those who have risen far enough in the social scale to have overcome such inhibitions. We shall be returning to these internal motivations in a later chapter. At this point we simply register the fact that as an external parameter economy generally means mass-production, and mass-production has a rhythmical aesthetic of its own.

Generally, but not always. For there is a much more venerable and more intriguing way of getting yourself housed cheaply: Do It Yourself. The urban poor in all countries where they exist live in three ways: in standardised municipal housing, in ghettoes owned by 'slumlords', and in the shanty towns, *barriadas* or *bidonvilles* they build themselves. So dehumanised and soulless is municipal housing, so humiliating and congested are the ghettoes, that in cities like Hong Kong and Lima and Caracas the step into one's own shanty is a step upwards, not only physically on to mountainsides where the air is clear and the view fine, but socially into a free world where the family can make its own mark, however modest, on the surface of the planet. If we are to take human need seriously as one of our parameters, we shall ignore this need for individuality in conditions requiring extreme economy at our peril, for we are in a situation in which it is going to transform itself rapidly from an unspoken need into a demand. Rather than let it run to seed in primitive muddle and squalor we shall then set about building the structures and the grids of services, both in the ground and in the air, in which it can take root and flower. This is another theme to which we shall be returning.

Last among the external parameters is the one that comes first in all the textbooks since Viollet-le-Duc: the decisive influence of means on ends.

It was for example the view of Patrick Geddes and after him Lewis Mumford that the whole of human history could be divided into an'eotechnic' era in which men used unconverted the materials provided by nature and the energy provided by winds and waters; a 'palaeotechnic' era in which both materials and energy were mined and manufactured in the form of iron and coal – so that the planet had to spend its capital instead of its income; and a 'neotechnic' era in which we revert to inexhaustible power resources such as the sun (nuclear energy) and the rivers and tides (electricity), and building materials become light and dry instead of heavy and wet.

In the elementary sense that building is the putting together of bits and pieces of material it is obvious that the nature of the material will influence the method of assembly and consequently the finished form. Every schoolboy knows that stone lintels mean short spans, wooden beams longer ones, steel joists longer still. The striking thing is not that technics influence architecture so much, but that they influence it so little. The pride of the cathedral builders was not to build within the crystalline ponderous nature of stone but to transcend it, if necessary by stretching its capabilities to breaking point. The purpose of Renaissance architects was to embody certain ideas, and the material they used to build with were as aesthetically neutral as the paint of Leonardo or the trees of Le Notre. Even the modern movement, in spite of all the talk about technical integrity, has yearned to treat concrete 'plastically' as though it were clay in the hands of a giant modeller, and has not hesitated to glue bricks on to the underside of concealed concrete beams. In the end, we do what we want.

All the same, we can hardly refuse to give technics its traditional place among the parameters. Whatever the mannerisms of the past and present, we still recognise them as mannerisms and in our more lucid moments react against them towards the logical unaffected structures that we like to think the engineers can show us how to build. Economy of means has an elegance (not to mention an economy) that appeals to the rational half of us, as well as to that puritanical conscience which has been said to be characteristic of architects for the last hundred years.

Within this generalisation one can perhaps distinguish one break-point in the otherwise consistent mutual interaction of technics with building. Until the technological revolution of the last few generations buildings were essentially shelters assembled out of a variety of components. You built your shelter which could be anything from a tent to a palace and then you carried to it water, fuel, food, messages, entertainers. In the course of the last century all these services have become piped and de-personalised, and it would now be more vivid to describe buildings as life-support systems which become operational through being plugged into a communal network of services visible and invisible. Here is a re-versal of roles: the services, which used to move around (mainly on two legs) have become fixtures; and the building (which used to symbolise stability) has become at least potentially and theoretic-ally as mobile as a caravan.

We can now summarise the external factors which individually have influenced and collectively should influence the form of build-ings – if we are right in assuming that we want them to please us. They are the user's spoken desires and unspoken needs, the climate and microclimate, the site and scene, the economics of investment, and the economics of structure and services by the full and rational exploitation of available techniques. If there had ever been a truly functional architecture, it would have emerged from these para-meters as inevitably as a weapons system from a defence specifica-tion. In reality weapons of war because they are totally insulated from market pressures are just about the only artefacts that do emerge in this way. Every other product has to be liked or at least admired if it is to be bought or used, and therefore has to be designed. And as soon as the designer comes on the scene we have the human mind to contend with, a vessel which contains all sorts of equipment not as yet analysable in terms of electrical circuits. If we are to understand architecture we have to look inside the mind of the architect, and this we do in the next chapter.

2

Images

I cast my net into their seas and wanted to
catch good fish; but I always pulled up
the head of some old god.   *Nietzsche*

The mind of the architect is a big room full of old furniture. Being human he has characteristic human compulsions, such as to bring order out of chaos, and to search for something new. 'The artist,' said Stravinsky, 'tries to find a cool place on the pillow.' And because he is a dreamer, his head is full of images.

Architecture deals in images, sometimes by inventing new ones, mostly by retailing old. This is an aboriginal form of communication, older than the written word. Long before it could be thought of as a machine for living in, a house had to be a place for feeling safe in: the womb, the cave, the fortress were our first habitats. The worker as he slams his front door at the end of the day returns to the womb. The child's image of the house, with this same front door, and the smoking chimney, and the windows that look out on the world like eyes, is above all an image of security, privacy and warmth. Other attributes are secondary.

The sources of this image are of course ethological as well as physiological. They derive, that is to say, from the territorial instincts of our animal ancestors and then from those of the tribe. The fortified village and the fortified manor are as ancient as the family hearth; they are places in which we may dominate a small world as well as retire from the great one. 'In defeat, defiance.'

Hence the pride in the bit of land, however minuscule, in the walled garden or the private kingdom. So with the collapse of the spacious and extrovert ideals of the Renaissance there occurred a romantic reaction to the castellated mansion and the secret garden, or to their scaled-down suburban versions. The mood is essentially one of withdrawal from the intellectual effort of the day to the comfort of the night, from the Apollonian to the Dionysian, from air to earth. Frank Lloyd Wright's prairie houses were a later manifestation, 'loving the ground' as he said, and so is all their rubble-chimneyed, deep-eaved, earth-coloured progeny. All dense pachydermatous buildings with rough exteriors and sunken openings are part of this tradition.

Part of it too, for all its elegance, is the fairytale silhouette of the fortified town, those marvellous images of the fifteenth-century manuscripts which so obsess the planner's imagination that he still thinks of the town as a sharp-cut jewel on a velvet landscape and believes it stands to reason that towns should have a 'hard edge' and recognisable 'gateways' – like the child who asks his father as they drive through Barnet or Bromley 'have we got to London yet?' It is this medieval image more than anything that has given suburbia, which is by definition extra-mural and un-confined, a bad name. Yet ever since the invention of gunpowder the hard line between town and country has been a myth. All the parameters point to an imperceptible transition; all the images of the city of our dreams forbid it.

Almost as ancient is the Great Concourse: the perfect circle of the tribe around its chief, starting on the threshing floor, ending in the stadium. Here either politics, drama or ritual sacrifice may be performed and the alternatives give the great mandala forms that house them a disconcerting ambivalence. On the whole, what takes place at the heart of the great concourse is tragedy or cruelty, direct or enacted: not much joy sounds in the roar of the crowd. So it is with some misgivings that one sees Christians moving out of their dark naves into these great floodlit arenas of confrontation – magnificent though their architecture has been, from Epidauros right through to Max Berg's *Jahrhunderthalle* and the bull-ring

14

at Mexico City. The stadia that spot the world like lunar craters would scarcely reassure any traveller from outer space about our societies.

Religion, we must remember, has its other side – the dark side represented by the shrine, the cell and the aedicule. Its origins are the tomb in the pyramid, the Hebrew Holy of Holies, the Orphic Mysteries and the Cave of the Delphic oracle. Primitive Christianity, hidden in the catacombs or making do with abandoned basilicae, was born as a Mystery and even in its medieval flowering was brought out to the people from a place of darkness behind a tall rood-screen or iconostasis or an impenetrable iron fence.

These images of darkness are as powerful in our subconscious as the images of light. Persephone commutes between the two, Orpheus pursues his cavernous quest through countless modern allegories, and Milton's imagery of Satan's realm, as pictured for example in the crepuscular lithographs of John Martin, comes to contemporary life in the cathedral-sized caverns opened up by the French speleologists. Piranesi's prisons are a translation of these experiences into Palladian terms, the salt mines of Wieliezka and the slate mines of Ffestiniog are equally romantic functionalist versions. Echoes are heard in Thompson's *City of Dreadful Night*, in Fritz Lang's sky-less *Metropolis* and in the first sequence of *Doctor Zhivago*.

Surfacing from Pluto's regions we find the daylight gods and goddesses still ensconced in caves, groves, grottoes, and wayside shrines. To the Greeks 'every cave and fountain is haunted by a nymph; in the ocean dwell the Nereids, in the mountain the Oread, the Dryad in the wood, and everywhere, in groves and marshes, on the pastures or the rocky heights, floating in the current of the streams or traversing untrodden snows, in the day at the chase or as evening closes in solitude fingering his flute, seen and heard by shepherds, alone or with his dancing train, is to be met the horned and goat-footed, the sunny-smiling Pan'.* These numinous crannies and currents of air would later be marked by the Christian Virgin in her glass-fronted shrine or by the Hindu

* G. Lowes Dickinson, *The Greek View of Life* (1896).

15

Ganesh, the elephant god, in his painted niche. It has even been suggested* that among the form-making elements of Gothic architecture (rather than among its decorative clichés) are these doll's houses or aedicules, each with its gabled canopy and saintly inhabitant. Certainly in the form of garden temples they were to be a favourite toy of the Italian Baroque and eventually the English Romantic landscapists, and there are vistas and arbours for which there still seems to us no really satisfactory alternative piece of furniture.

But the gods' ultimate abode is the mountain-top. Of this the most powerful architectural image is the Indo-Chinese pagoda with its dizzy and superhuman steps – their slope at roughly the same angle as the summit cone of Snowdon. The Bayon temple at Angkor is worn and weathered to a mountain shape, on which every rock-face turns out to be the huge face of a god. The mountain to our ancestors spelt security as well as divinity, security from the terrors of marsh and forest, and there seems no doubt that the architect's yearning to build high, so often attributed to an ambition to leave a monument to himself, and the tendency of all of us to goggle at skyscrapers, are in fact expressions of the mountain-mystique of primitive man. To Pugin, of course, 'the vertical principle being an acknowledged emblem of the Resurrection' it was unnecessary to look beyond the Christian era to these pagan fears and desires.

Most people when they think of height think, like the early American skyscraper builders, of Gothic, the great mystery at the heart of western architecture. It is mysterious because we know enough of the medieval mind to know that what their architecture means to us is not what it meant to them. Yet what it meant to them can only be guessed at, because its builders never explained themselves: they had no Vitruvius, Alberti or Palladio.

One can eliminate misconceptions. Panofsky has shown that neither pure structural logic nor pure fancy lay at the core of the architecture of the cathedrals.

* By Sir John Summerson.

With reference to twelfth and thirteenth-century architecture, the alternative, 'all is function – all is illusion', is as little valid as would be, with reference to twelfth and thirteenth-century philosophy, the alternative 'all is search for truth – all is intellectual gymnastics and oratory'. The ribs of Caen and Durham began by saying something before being able to do it. The flying buttresses of Caen and Durham, still hidden beneath the roofs of the side aisles, began by doing something before being permitted to say so. Ultimately, the flying buttress learned to talk, the rib learned to work, and both learned to proclaim what they were doing in language more circumstantial, explicit, and ornate than was necessary for mere efficiency; and this applies also to the conformation of the piers and the tracery which had been talking as well as working all the time.*

He sees the great cathedrals of the Ile de France as manifestations, deliberately dramatised, of the supremely synthetic power of reason, manifestations both comprehensive (which made their immense size expressive) and hierarchical (which made their clear articulation of parts expressive), and he demonstrates how the development of High Gothic to its logically perfect statement in the nave of St Denys (1230) occurred in exactly the same dialectical fashion as a scholastic disputation.

This is as close as we are likely to get to the cause of the cathedrals. But it gives no account, indeed attempts none, of their consequences, which turned out entirely different. For one thing, the classic achievement of the early thirteenth century had neither staying power nor spreading power. It was never matched or even understood outside France, and even in France it soon degenerated into rigid academicism on the one hand or mannerism on the other. Certainly the English romantics, who were later to conceive such a passionate and proprietary attachment to what they believed to be Gothic architecture, never penetrated the minds that had invented it and would have been out of sympathy with them if they had.

Their images of Gothic, and by descent ours, were as various as Gothic itself. The logic and clarity which made it, even in Ruskin's

* Erwin Panofsky, *Gothic Architecture and Scholasticism* (1948).

17

opinion 'the only rational architecture', were the qualities least often remembered. More characteristic is the vivid reference in *The Stones of Venice* to an architecture which

smites an uncouth animation out of the rocks . . . and heaves into the darkened air the piles of iron buttress and rugged wall, instinct with the work of an imagination as wild and wayward as the northern sea; creatures of ungainly shape and rigid limb, but full of wolfish life; fierce as the winds that beat and changeful as the clouds that shade them.*

Here, near the end of the Revival, is the image which had ushered in its beginning – a dark image, full of mystery, primitive, northern, honest, unaffected, 'English' (no Revivalist ever admitted it was French). Partly these attributions were due to the Revival occurring in an island whose Gothic architecture was indeed more often than not romantic in silhouette, disorderly in form and much decayed. Partly they can be accounted for by a compulsive need to escape from the gracious living of the eighteenth century and the materialism and heartless industrialism of the nineteenth. Like most drugs, Gothic was an affectation before it became an addiction: its negative significance as a protest, most effectively expressed in Pugin's *Contrasts*, always outweighed its positive value as a generator of works of art.

This was largely because the protest was a moral one. It was Pugin's conviction, and Ruskin's, as Clark has put it, that 'certain right states of temper and moral feeling were the magic powers by which all architecture has been produced'.† A sensation of superior virtue is a common incentive among architects, but it does not belong among the images; it is more often, as we have seen, felt by those who have given a lot of attention to the parameters.

The 'Gothic' image, not entirely shorn of its moral overtones, is as powerful today as it ever was, and is as effective as ever as an escape mechanism from an official and commercial architecture that is felt to be excessively dull, rational and repetitive. In a lecture given by Rudolf Steiner in 1921 we seem to be looking

* John Ruskin, *The Stones of Venice* (1853).
† Kenneth Clark, *The Gothic Revival* (1928).

back to the Gothic of the cathedrals as well as forward to the fashion for Gaudi, for the early Mendelsohn, and for the expressionism of the 20s, to the 'New Brutalism' of the 50s and to the plastic forms of Candela and Utzon.

The entire building [he is speaking of the first Goetheanum at Dornach], the whole architecture, has been conceived as a totality, and each part has been conceived in its proper place as it must be at that place. . . . The attempt has been made to change from mere geometric mechanical architecture to organic forms. The building had to be created according to the same innermost laws that are followed in reciting, in producing mystery plays, and according to which eurhythmy is now performed. As one can experience within oneself the whole configuration of the Gothic in the buttresses, in the groin vault etc., one can also learn to feel that inner shaping or form-creating of nature, which takes place in any organic growing process.*

And finally:

Harmony, reigning over all things, regulating all the things of our lives, is the spontaneous, indefatigable and tenacious quest of man animated by a single force: the sense of the divine.

These last words are not Steiner's but Le Corbusier's, and with them we may turn our attention to that 'geometric mechanical architecture' against which the Gothic protest was directed.

Three powerful emotions moulded the architecture of the Renaissance: a sense of wonder, a sense of order, and a sense of space. And while eventually they all acted together, they emerged in that order, and in that order I will try to define them.

Because we still, though only just, inhabit a world whose future could be better than its past, it is impossible for us to imagine what it must have been like to live in the reverse situation, among the colossal ruins of a more sophisticated and more powerful culture than one's own. The fact that the ruins of Rome had stood for a thousand years, the length of time that divides us from Edward the Confessor, far from weakening their influence, drove it more deeply into the European unconscious, which it seems

* Rudolf Steiner, from a lecture given in Berne, 29 June 1921.

permanently to inhabit, emerging as numinous as ever in the opium dreams of Coleridge and de Quincey, Baudelaire and Cocteau.*

> J'ai longtemps habité sous de vastes portiques
> Que les soleils marins teignaient de mille feux,
> Et que leur grands piliers, droits et majestueux,
> Rendaient pareils, le soir, aux grottes basaltiques.†

Even Palladio, in a spirit that reminds us of Ruskin's view of Gothic, saw these 'enormous ruins as a shining and sublime testimony to Roman virtue and greatness'.

Alberti might study and experiment with Roman forms, Serlio reduce them to formulae, Palladio revivify them, Michelangelo distort them, but the sense of awe that they first inspired in Petrarch clung to them right through to the eighteenth century (as we can see from Piranesi's Roman engravings and the follies and eye-catchers they inspired all over Europe). The cult of ruins,‡ whether classic or gothic or abstract, is a notable element in the now well-documented English picturesque tradition. Its ingredients are escapism from a well-ordered society, certain optical novelties and all the associations of a literary kind which are the stock-in-trade of romanticim. The cult is as popular as ever, if one is to judge from John Piper's war paintings and the subsequent fashion for turning bombed churches into gardens§ and building modern houses at the feet of the Doric porticoes of demolished country houses. It seems hard to get these columns out of the system.

The first flush of enthusiasm for Roman architecture was as

---

* Alethea Hayter, *Opium and the Romantic Imagination* (1968).
† Baudelaire, *Les Fleurs du Mal*.
‡ See Rose Macaulay, *The Pleasure of Ruins* (1953).
§ See Le Corbusier's plans for St Dié cathedral. 'I propose to make the charred and ruined cathedral a living torch of architecture; to take deferent charge of the misfortunes which have struck it, and make it a perpetual witness of the tragic event for the rest of time. The roof has fallen in, and the choir and transepts, cut to pieces against the sky, allow through their jagged shreds of red stone a glimpse of mountains and of the waving foliage of great trees.'

20

unscholarly and unsystematic as the Georgians' enthusiasm for Gothic, and it was not until the early sixteenth century that Vitruvius was republished and the classical grammar of architecture put out for universal use. It was at this time too that the Pythagoreans got to work on those elegant mathematical constructions which embraced the solar system, the human body, the musical octave and the ground plans of classical churches and villas in a single universal harmony. This great poetic concept of Divine Order, which still on a starlight night brings the music of the spheres almost to the threshold of audibility, has never quite faded from the European consciousness. When for the hundredth time philistine committees express their dislike for architecture in Hume's useful half-truth 'beauty is in the eye of the beholder', architects can even now persuade themselves that there must be some Platonic secret by which they can prove their critics wrong.

Gallantly coming to their rescue, Le Corbusier launched his Modulor in 1950 like a belated Atlantic liner under the banner of Mathematics – 'that majestic structure conceived by man to grant him comprehension of the Universe'. But by now any such comprehension was beyond the capacity of physicists, let alone architects, and Corb had to content himself with a couple of simple arithmetical series having some rough relationship with the dimensions of the human body. It was originally conceived for Latin bodies, and a Mark II was later rushed out for Anglo-Saxons, who were at that time thought to be taller, but there is no Modulor for women, least of all for Indian women. Nor did either Modulor work very well when applied to familiar masterpieces.

An examination of these measurements [of the Parthenon] can lead to a thousand conclusions . . . in those circumstances the reading of the figures was fairly encouraging, with the help of convictions, and a few inches (or millimetres) suggested by pure faith.*

It need hardly be said that this is not the sort of mathematics that has given us comprehension of the universe. That is why we can have no hesitation in placing this and all such golden rules (as distinct from modular systems of pure convenience) not among

---

* Le Corbusier, *Le Modulor* (1950).

the parameters but among the images. There, solid and foursquare at the back of our minds, even though its rules lack any universal sanction, is the image of an architecture 'proportionable according to the rules, masculine and unaffected'. Thus Inigo Jones, with Vitruvius and Palladio in mind. And it is interesting to note that a century and a half later, when satiated with stylistic whimsy men sought to revive the pure architecture of the Periclean golden age, it was in similar terms that they commended it. This same association with manliness, purity and republican virtue also led to its adoption as the national style of the youthful United States.

The third legacy of the Renaissance is the sense of space. If you have crossed from the medieval alleys of Old Delhi into the Renaissance vistas of New, or sat in darkness at that moment when the little black and white cinema screen exploded into Cinerama, you will have felt some faint echo of the spatial revelation of that age. Wittkower* has shown how the medieval cathedral, with its jagged Latin cross plan-form symbolising an agonising victory over surrounding Chaos, gave place to the calm dome of the Renaissance, symbolising the Cosmos, a relaxed, immutable and universal Order with man at its centre in the image of God (the rounded capital letters themselves contributing a certain stability). Thus Buddha, we are told, stepped at birth into the centre of an eight-petalled lotus and in a 'symbolic gesture of survey' gazed into the ten directions of space – eight horizontal, one upward and one down.

Much of this was of course a rediscovery. Plutarch speaks of Rome as *urbs quadrata*, its walls a perfect circle described by the plough of Romulus, which he lifted to allow gateways at the four points of the compass, and Le Corbusier has a telling illustration of the great round section of the Pantheon, easily outspanning the successive attempts of the cathedral builders, standing, he says, 'for a plain and objective state of mind'. And of course we have the impeccable symmetry of Peking and Angkor to confirm that the thrust of the central axis is a human and not a specifically European invention. Even longer ago, 'it is related of the Socratic

* F. Wittkower, *Architectural Principles in the Age of Humanism* (1949).

philosopher Aristippus that, being shipwrecked and cast ashore on the coast of the Rhodians, he observed geometrical figures drawn thereon, and cried out to his companions: "Let us be of good cheer, for I see the traces of Man.""*

The achievement of the Renaissance (or more specifically the Baroque) was to extend this geometry over the whole landscape. The Greeks, if we may guess at their intentions as we walk through the ruins of Delphi and Ephesus, had created the urban stroll or processional way, an experience full of architectural incident, embracing the landscape in outward glimpses but imposing no mechanical order upon it: a lost art until Nash in London and Repton in the English countryside recovered it almost unconsciously. Rome had never possessed this kinetic vision, dumping down its vast columned platitudes, even in as sophisticated an example as Hadrian's villa, in no intelligible relation with one another – its most significant contribution an interpretation between indoor and outdoor space which was also to remain a lost art for millennia.

It can only have been the invention of perspective which broke the barrier by means of its tantalising vanishing point, first exploited by Sixtus V in setting up his obelisks and so creating the spatial armature for Baroque Rome, a device in due course to be adapted by Louis XIII, l'Enfant, John Burley Griffin, Lutyens, *et al.*, until it became the prestige symbol for the colonial city. Already in the original Sistine example the vistas so created were too long for comfort, either of the eye or the feet. The vanishing point vanished into the mist and the walk to reach it was boring as well as exhausting.

It was when le Notre finally projected his great shaft of space, as Edmund Bacon calls it,† through the walls of Paris and headed it for the horizon that the Renaissance mastery of space reached its consummation: no longer now a way of arranging buildings but a way of assimilating the landscape. The image of the walled city, the island in the dangerous wilderness, exploded overnight and

* Vitruvius.
† Edmund Bacon, *Design of Cities* (1967).

in its place the geometry of direct human communication steadily netted the habitable world, superimposing its grids indifferently on the plains of India and the prairies of the American West. The landscape comes under command; in Paris, in London, in Bath, tall windows frame unlimited horizons and along the English coasts and in the Irish countryside terraces of houses are put down imperturbably in the windy fields. 'Under such conditions,' concludes Le Corbusier, 'the mind is calm; ideas of planning on a noble scale can then make themselves heard.' And he rounds off his *City of Tomorrow* with a portrait of Louis xiv.

In thus taming the accessible landscape, the Renaissance consciously or unconsciously thrust aside the most striking aspect of the land surface of the globe, that it is untameable. Perhaps that is why baroque vistas, whether urban or rural, were elaborately canalised, and buildings or trees were used to wall them in rather than as objects in themselves. It was one of Le Corbusier's great insights, probably derived, as Scully has shown, from his love of Greece, that even the most powerful statements of man are made in a setting which he can never hope to master.

In the baroque, as at the Spanish Stairs or at Versailles, all, even nature, is controlled by the human will. At Chandigarh the human act in the building, itself harsher and more elemental than baroque opera could have imagined, is exposed to the reciprocal action of the natural world. A more tragic view of human fate than that held by the early eighteenth century prevails. The balance that results has the effect of a pact between antagonists. There is no outcome, no victory, only the splendid, precarious treaty and the blinding light of the recognition of what the realities are.*

We had not of course seen the last of the medieval backlash. The Gothic reaction against order was to be followed, later in the Victorian era, by a reaction against space. Camillo Sitte and Raymond Unwin were the first of a long succession of German and English writers to discover in the winding lanes and charming juxtapositions of medieval towns subtleties, whether accidental or deliberate we shall never know, totally remote from the intentions,

* Vincent Scully Jr, *Modern Architecture: the Architecture of Democracy* (1961).

or even the capabilities, of the Renaissance. By the second half of the twentieth century the necessity and the technique of pedestrianising parts of towns had attracted the attention of English romantics to the decaying nooks and crannies, the galaxy of small spaces and great steps and subtle slopes and changes of texture and colour and focus that Italians had always taken for granted, now for the first time photographed from the one telling viewpoint for their albums of townscape lore.

Seen through a mist of chianti and sun-oil, the eternal dream of the Mediterranean rose again in the northern imagination, and we

> saw in sleep old palaces and towns
> quivering within the wave's intenser day,
> all overgrown with azure moss and flowers
> so sweet, the sense faints picturing them:

But never until now had anybody dismissed the palaces and concentrated on the slums, happily ignoring the clear experience that such felicities were untranslatable.

Over this same last century, and for similar reasons, the venerable ideal of the leafy suburb, for so long denigrated by intellectuals, had come into its own again. This leap over the wall was at least as old as imperial Rome, when every garrison town had its extramural *colonia*, and we have Alberti's word for it that 'there is a vast deal of satisfaction in a convenient retreat near the town, where a man is at liberty to do just what he pleases'. The hollyhocks by the cottage wall, the wavy rooflines, the backcloth of elms, the vertical column of wood-smoke smudging a sunset sky full of rooks, the pony club and all the other clubs, the loyalties and dramas of a hundred Hollywood soap operas – all this reassuring imagery lay and still lies at the back of the minds of realtors and customers the length and breadth of the affluent societies, however raw and impoverished its actualities. Thus Herbert Gans in his apologia for Levittown,* latest and rawest of the innumerable progeny of Blaise Hamlet, Bedford Park and Hampstead, has no reservations whatever.

* Herbert J. Gans, *The Levittowners: Anatomy of Suburbia* (1967).

The community may displease the professional city planner and the intellectual defender of cosmopolitan culture, for Levittown permits most of its residents to be what they want to be – to centre their lives around the home and the family, to be among neighbors whom they can trust, to find friends to share leisure hours, and to participate in organizations that provide sociability and opportunity to be of service to others.

By any yardstick one chooses, Levittowners treat their fellow residents more ethically and more democratically than did their parents. They also live a 'fuller' and 'richer' life. Their culture may be less subtle and sophisticated than that of the intellectual, their family life less healthy than that advocated by psychiatrists, and their politics less thoughtful and democratic than political philosophers' – yet all of these are superior to what prevailed among the working and lower middle classes of past generations.

Like the rest of the anti-rational reaction, the suburban image is clearly more moral than aesthetic, and none the less powerful for that.

Curiously enough, the same is true of its exact opposite, the Machine Aesthetic, to which we must now turn our attention. The notion that steel structures were beautiful didn't occur to anybody for at least half a century after their first appearance in Europe and America. As late as the 1920s Max Beerbohm would lower the blinds of his carriage window as his train passed Sydenham, and the Eiffel Tower was considered a vulgar horror by men of taste. The usual argument was the one now used against rocketry – that a thing isn't necessarily desirable just because it is possible. As for the great industrial buildings of the Victorian era, these were given a wide berth as dark Satanic mills until well after the Second World War. But then the English were the last people in Europe to absorb the image of their own industrial revolution. Many would still subscribe to Sir William Chambers' view of industrial buildings as 'objects of the horrid kind'.

The first image-builders of the machine age were the young Italian Futurists, innocent harbingers of fascism, victims of the First World War, ancestors of all our neo-technic and jet-age fantasists from the Russian constructivists of the 1920s through to Buckminster Fuller and the megastructures and comic-strip aesthetics of the 60s. In Marinetti's original manifesto of 1909 and in Sant'Elia's Messaggio of 1914 we find for the first time nearly all the magic incantations of the modern movement, later to be put into cooler and more sophisticated terms by Oud, Moholy-Nagy and Le Corbusier.

Thus Marinetti:*

We declare that the splendour of the world has been enriched by a new beauty – the beauty of speed. A racing car with its bonnet draped with exhaust-pipes like fire-breathing serpents – a roaring racing car, rattling along like a machine gun, is more beautiful than the winged victory of Samothrace.

We will sing of the stirring of great crowds – workers, pleasure-seekers, rioters – and the confused sea of colour and sound as revolution sweeps through a modern metropolis. We will sing the midnight fervour of arsenals and shipyards blazing with electric moons; insatiable stations swallowing the smoking serpents of their trains; factories hung from the clouds by the twisted threads of their smoke; bridges flashing like knives in the sun, giant gymnasts that leap over rivers; adventurous steamers that scent the horizon; deep-chested locomotives that paw the ground with their wheels, like stallions harnessed with steel tubing: the easy flight of aeroplanes, their propellers beating the wind like banners, with a sound like the applause of a mighty crowd.

These men enjoy, in short, a life of power between walls of iron or crystal; they have furniture of steel, twenty times lighter and cheaper than ours. They are free at last from the examples of fragility and softness offered by wood and fabrics with their rural ornaments. . . . Heat, humidity and ventilation regulated by a brief pass of the hand, they feel the fullness and solidity of their own will . . .

and Sant'Elia:

We must invent and rebuild *ex novo* our modern city like an immense and tumultuous shipyard, active, mobile and everywhere dynamic, and the modern building like a gigantic machine. Lifts must no longer hide away like solitary worms in the stairwells, but the stairs – now useless

---

* See Reyner Banham, *Theory and Design in the First Machine Age* (1960), for all these quotations.

– must be abolished, and the lifts must swarm up the façade like serpents of glass and iron. The house of cement, iron, and glass, without carved or painted ornament, rich only in the inherent beauty of its lines and modelling, extraordinarily brutish in its mechanical simplicity, as big as needs dictate, and not merely as zoning rules permit, must rise from the brink of a tumultuous abyss; the street which, itself, will no longer lie like a doormat at the level of the thresholds, but plunge storeys deep into the earth, gathering up the traffic of the metropolis connected for necessary transfers to metal cat-walks and high-speed conveyor belts. And I affirm

That the new architecture is the architecture of cold calculation, temerious boldness and simplicity, the architecture of reinforced concrete, iron, glass, textile fibres and all those replacements for wood, stone and brick that make for the attainment of maximum elasticity and lightness.

The unifying idea in all this is the concept of modern man as a new kind of person, of modernism as a heroic adventure, of the architect as a tough-minded pioneer sharing the risks and fantasies of science and science fiction, of the *avant-garde* as the standard-bearer of *l'esprit nouveau* and the only fit place for a young man to be seen in. Thus Le Corbusier (in *Le Modulor*):

Engineers and architects were assembled, some wily like foxes in the thicket of technique, others devoted and impassioned like true fighters for a cause – the cause of our civilisation.

Never before had the generally shy, inarticulate architect been called upon to see himself like this.

Within this powerful central image, one can identify six main themes in the imagery of twentieth-century modernist architecture:

Speed
Steel
Concrete
Transparency
Impermanence
Geometry

Speed is our great life-enhancer and reassurance, or so the copywriters believe, and there seems no doubt that westernised man in his more expansive moments sees himself as this smoothly turned-out fast-moving executive, a master of all the electronic aids, that posterity will no doubt class with the noble savage as one of the great myths of history. As a form-maker, speed has produced the many potent images of multi-level circulation, the monorail, the multiple traffic node, a whole architecture of movement systems that wears its guts outside its skin, and out in the landscape the gentle curve of the railway and the grander sweeps of the motor-way, not to mention the great dead expanses of the airport. '*La beauté de l' aeroport, c'est la splendeur de l' espace. . . .*'* At the other end of the design scale it is responsible for the streamlined peram-bulator and other jokes. Speed nowadays has become explosive, and we shall be returning to its fallout in a later chapter.

Steel, or originally iron, is the prima donna of modernism. Great crowds applauded its first appearances under the direction of original geniuses like Telford and Stephenson, and by 1860 Viollet-le-Duc was suggesting that 'a practical architect might not un-naturally conceive the idea of erecting a vast edifice whose frame should be entirely of iron'. Yet the first American skyscrapers, those prodigious orange cages clamorous with riveters, could not emerge until the electric elevator was developed in the 1880s. And when they did the architects were too snobbish to associate the material with art and too innumerate to master its technology. It was relegated to a purely supporting and servant role, a Cin-derella banned from the drawing-room. Seen for a suggestive moment through a mist of scaffolding, and for that brief time infinitely more beautiful than the final stone-clad building would ever be, it offered to the imagination of Mies van der Rohe a skeletal architecture that could be 'almost nothing'. In his hands in the 1940s it was to acquire almost the opposite characteristics – solemn, classic and terribly expensive.

Concrete in the course of its shorter history has built up an even wider range of imagery. Historically this has been in part a reflec-tion of the usual three-stage assimilation of a new material:

* Le Corbusier, *Oeuvre Complète* (1946).

primitive, when it adopts the aesthetic of an old one, mature, when it has learnt to exploit its own characteristics, and mannerist, when it breaks its own rules and goes for effects for their own sake. To this one must add the peculiar ambivalence of the material, combining the physique of a jumper and a weight lifter, so that once past its primitive phase with Perret it could be seen simultaneously stripped, athletic and cool in the bridges of Maillart, feminine with Nervi, masculine with Tange, and mannerist with Candela. Le Corbusier, the great admirer of Michelangelo, played that master's part in the process, riding the crest of classical maturity, then leading the plunge into mannerism. If there is a survivor of all this, it is the image of a grey, rough, abrasive, muscular material, the masculine element in a powerfully heterosexual relationship with the elegancies and transparencies of glass.

Transparency has always been of the essence of modernism. At its first revelation in 1851 a German observer* had no doubt of its potentialities:

In contemplating the first great building [the Crystal Palace] which was not of solid masonry construction spectators were not slow to realise that here the standards by which architecture had hitherto been judged no longer held good.

We see a delicate network of lines without any clues by means of which we might judge their distance from the eye or the real size. The side walls are too far apart to be embraced in a single glance. Instead of moving from the wall at one end to that at the other, the eye sweeps along an unending perspective which fades into the horizon. We cannot tell if this structure towers a hundred or a thousand feet above us, or whether the roof is a flat platform or is built up from a succession of ridges, for there is no play of shadows to enable our optic nerves to gauge the measurements.

If we let our gaze travel downward it encounters the blue-painted lattice girders. At first these occur only at wide intervals: then they range closer and closer together until they are interrupted by a dazzling band of light – the transept – which dissolves into a distant background where all materiality is blended into the atmosphere. . . . It is sober

* Lothar Bucher, quoted by Siegfried Giedion in *Space, Time and Architecture* (1941).

economy of language if I call the spectacle incomparable and fairylike. It is a Midsummer Night's Dream seen in the clear light of midday.

A century earlier, Sir William Chambers had ruled as follows:

Palladio observes that windows should not be broader than one quarter of the room nor narrower than one fifth of it; and that their height should be twice and one sixth of their breadth. But, as in one house there are large, middling and small rooms, and all the windows of one floor must nevertheless be of one size, he prefers those rooms of which the length exceeds the breadth in the ratio of 5 to 3 for determining the dimensioning of the windows.*

This was roughly what the Gothic revival and the search for a new architecture were all about, and we may note in passing that one may interpret Gothic not solely as a brilliant system for enclosing space but also as a brilliant system for admitting light, though of course through glass that was translucent and not transparent.

With transparency for the first time man's dwelling in the cold north ceased to be a retreat from nature and became an observatory – a significant by-product of the Enlightenment. He could if he chose (though he did not so choose till the 1950s) let the woodland be his only visible wall, with nothing between him and the snow but double glazing. More important aesthetically, plate glass revealed far more effectively than stained glass had done the essentially vertebrate nature of modern, as of medieval, architecture. The floating planes of floor and roof long since adumbrated in the imagination of Mondrian, Wright and Rietveld finally became airborne in the Barcelona Pavilion and *Falling Water*; and the prismatic glass skyscraper, first modelled by Mies in 1921, flourished and produced its innumerable offspring. Not only the transparency of plate glass, but its reflections and ambiguities, plus the multiple viewpoints and interpenetrations of cubist painting, seem between them to have finished off Renaissance Man with his static perspective and boring shaft of space. It was the artists of the Bauhaus, and in particular Moholy-Nagy, who first explored what he correctly called the New Vision and defined thus:

* *Treatise on Civil Architecture* (1759).

Formerly the architect made from visible, measurable and well-proportioned volumes building masses, calling this 'space creation'. But real spatial experiences rest in simultaneous interpenetration of inside and outside, above and beneath, and on the in and out flowing of space relationship, on the invisible play of forces present in the materials. Thus a present-day space creation does not consist in putting together heavy building masses, nor in the formation of hollow bodies, nor in the relative positions of well-arranged volumes. . . . Space creation is to-day much more an interweaving of parts of spaces, which are anchored for the most part in invisible but clearly traceable relations, moving in all directions, and in the fluctuating play of forces.*

Proving incidentally the difficulty of putting any sensual experience into words.

With insubstantiality went impermanence. 'The fundamental characteristics of Futurist architecture,' wrote Sant'Elia, 'will be expendability and transience. Our houses will last less time than we do, and every generation will have to make its own.' This was the first time in human history that architecture, which had always been a symbolic denial of the brevity of human life, set up impermanence as one of its targets. It was not an easy one to hit, because buildings which will last a generation will last a lot longer: even in our richest societies their economic lifetime lies somewhere between their functional obsolescence and their structural decay. But the image of the system-built, adjustable, expendable dwelling, clipped into a three-dimensional grid of services and then unclipped and replaced, is still very much alive. Even if buildings are not as 'light and dry' as they pretend, it is inherent in this image that they seem so, perching on the landscape like gulls, not growing out of it like plants. The rusticated plinth is suppressed or pushed into the shadows so that the superstructure hovers clear of the ground.

Last among the images of the first half of the twentieth century has been the grid itself, that relentless criss-cross which led Steinberg to represent a modern office building by a piece of graph paper. This was no part of the ideology of the founding fathers of

* L.Moholy-Nagy, *The New Vision* (1939).

modernism, all of whom, from Morris and Mackintosh in England to Behrens, Gropius and Berlage in Germany and Holland, had handicraft connections of one sort or another. For the initial switchover from romantic to diagrammatic architecture we must look to Mondrian and the Dutch *de Stijl* group in the First World War, and for its worldwide acceptance in the 1920s as the central characteristic of the International Style to Le Corbusier.

The laws of gravity seem to resolve for us the conflict of forces and to maintain the universe in equilibrium; as a result of this we have the vertical. The horizon gives us the horizontal, the line of the transcendental plane of immobility. . . . The right angle therefore has superior rights over other angles; it is unique and it is constant. In order to work, man has need of constants. Without them he could not put one foot before the other. The right angle is, it may be said, the essential and sufficient instrument of action because it enables us to determine space with absolute exactness.*

This last over-simplification had been good enough for every colonial power that had to lay out new towns, from the Romans through to the Americans. Le Corbusier relied on it totally for his Contemporary City of Three Million Inhabitants, ignoring his own inconsistency, as between

Man walks in a straight line because he has a goal and knows where he is going.

and

A straight street is extremely boring to walk through.

In its final presentation the Contemporary City comprised a rectangular grid of streets and buildings (not without a few Beaux Arts vistas) superimposed upon a lower level of English-style parklands with winding paths, and this survived into the built form of Chandigarh, within a vaguely anthropomorphic central concept derived from the Modulor. It never worked, because pedestrians used the streets and not the footpaths, and the straight streets were indeed extremely boring, for the motorist dodging the bullock carts as well as for those few pedestrians who thought in such

* Le Corbusier, *The City of Tomorrow*, trans. F. Etchells (1929).

terms. These larger questions of urban geometry will re-appear in a later chapter.

Meanwhile, the graph-paper elevation has proved good business: in the world market for mass-produced prefabricated curtain walls, the pioneers have certainly got what they asked for.

Le Corbusier called his first masterly block of glass-walled flats *Clarté*, and his most beautiful single house *Les Heures Claires*, and his evocation of this image of clarity and translucence has never been excelled. 'Here,' he proclaimed, 'bathed in light, stands the modern city. . . . Their outlines softened by distance, the sky-scrapers raise immense geometrical façades, all of glass, and in them is reflected the blue glory of the sky. An overwhelming sensation: immense and radiant prisms.' But we cannot leave the image of the modern city at that high point of radiance and optimism. The cities we live in are just not like this, and fifty years after Le Corbusier wrote there seems no prospect that they ever will be, because *men* are not like this. As William James sensibly put it:

> In this real world of sweat and dirt, it seems to me that when a view of things is 'noble', that ought to count as a presumption against its truth, and as a philosophic disqualification.

Faced with this dull fact, romantics are apt to plunge into the opposite extreme. It was the Scottish biologist Patrick Geddes who first applied to cities those various Greek neologisms from eopolis through parisitopolis, pathopolis and megalopolis, to necropolis, which Lewis Mumford was later to darken into a nightmare progression. For the dream of an *urbs mirabilis* is a dream of the unattainable, and its whole force derives from its contrast with the diseased reality. This reality, in all its complexities, has a tragic grandeur of its own.

> Now [writes Jonathan Miller], with the symptoms of confusion, decay and upheaval at each street corner, the image of the city is perhaps the last model to which we might refer in trying to give ourselves a symbol of the unchanging order of the universe.
>
> [The city has become] a metaphor of hell . . . a secular inferno in which crime and punishment were confused in episodes of turbulent

34

misery. . . . But at the same time if the city became a metaphor for wrong-doing and its punishment it also became the great image of fantasy and insanity. Once again Dickens is the master of this insight. His London is full of people deranged by the alienations of the great city, people pursuing self-destructive obsessions. It was no longer possible to think of Bedlam as something set apart from the city. The street and the alleyway were the wards of this extended asylum and of course as the surrealists began to realise at the turn of the century the visual images provided by the city were often stranger and more florid than the fantasies of its maddest inhabitants. The city is a huge portfolio of visual paradox and we see how the artifice of the original city has now become an artifice within an artifice – stage set for an urban reality that has never actually been realised. The citizen as actor. The townspeople as scenery. A huge Pirandellian farce – six million characters in search of an absconded author.*

In this image, the great city only survives in the negative role of a kind of squalid undergrowth out of which rise on their delicate steel legs the megastructures of the future. Isozaki, the Japanese 'metabolist', in a metaphor of renewal, draws gigantic Doric ruins, slung between which constructivist steel sky-structures thread their way; and the Smithsons have the same image:

. . . a new way of living in the city must nearly always expect to lace-in between existing building and mesh over existing road and service networks. Their function is renewal of the dying centres and derelict areas among railway viaducts and old industrial sites. The 'elements' can expect little help from their surroundings in terms of environment but must by their unblemishable newness carry the whole load of responsibility for renewal in themselves.†

This is of course a travesty of what people really feel about cities. Even the worst English examples command a sort of wry affection, and this amounts to a cult in the writings of Jane Jacobs and the townscapists of the London *Architectural Review*. The Futurist image of the past as a rubbish heap is plainly untypical not merely of what we feel now but of what people have felt in the

* Jonathan Miller in a broadcast (1968).
† A. and P. Smithson, *Urban Structuring* (1967).

past itself. Twice in modern European history it has been through images of the past – of Rome or Greece or Gothic – that imagination has escaped from a rotten present into what seemed a better future.

Images of the past, images of the future. Images of darkness, images of light. Contemplating this crushing load of imagery humped around in the mind of the architect, which seemed to get more dense and diverse with every year that passed, it is hardly surprising that people should have tried to dump the lot. The theory of 'doing without', the theory that by devoted and undivided attention to the parameters one could dispense with the images, the often quoted yet scarcely meaningful tag of Keats – 'Beauty is truth, truth beauty' – the theory that in the 1930s came to be called Functionalism, has by now had a fairly long and lively history, at which we must now take a good look.

3

The Iconoclasts

The earliest text of functionalism is probably this plain statement by the French neo-classicist J. N. L. Durand (1760–1834):

Public and private usefulness, and the happiness and preservation of mankind, are the aims of architecture. . . . Thus one should not strive to make a building pleasing, since if one concerns oneself solely with the fulfilment of practical requirements, it is impossible that it should not be pleasing.

Brave words, yet their author never attempted to implement them. Still less did his predecessors Boullée and Ledoux, with their Platonic solid geometry and sombre imagery: practical requirements were about the last consideration to enter their minds. Even the more domesticated Soane was as pure an aesthete as ever spun a compass, and the common claim that he might have fathered modern architecture if the Gothic Revival had not supervened leaves out of account most of the heredity of modernism.

It was Summerson's judgement that:

Should anyone attempt to construct a theory of modern architecture in harmony with the conditions of thought prevailing today [1947], he will discover no starting point so firm, no backgrounds so solid, as that provided by Eugène Viollet-le-Duc.[*]

Viollet was not in fact the first to investigate Gothic structure, nor the first to call for a new architecture exploiting new materials. Willis on the first count and Pickett on the second, both writing

[*] Sir John Summerson 'Viollet-le-Duc and the Rational Point of View', in *Heavenly Mansions* (1949).

in England in the 1840s, were ahead of him. But he was the first to embody these fairly common preoccupations in the theory of architecture which we now call Functionalism.

Motivated negatively by a passionate contempt for the *Ecole des Beaux Arts* and positively by an equally passionate love for Gothic architecture, he can correctly be called an iconoclast because he was the first to turn a deliberately blind, though not a cold, eye to the imagery of Gothic and to construct a theory of design based solely on what he believed to be its structural principles. And he used this theory not to prop up Gothic but to postulate a new architecture. His *Entretiens* of the 1860s are full of functionalist statements that are not just asides in a theory of aesthetics but are the basic texts of a theory of design. Thus:

> We reflect deeply on what we are doing and consult our reason only, without concerning ourselves about traditions or time-hallowed forms. . . . Ought we not in building rather to consider the complicated requirements of our civilisation than how to combine styles of architecture? . . . The nature of materials not employed formerly oblige us to employ new forms.

And, most classically:

> Beauty . . . is the true and fitly chosen expression . . . of the physical and moral requirements we have to satisfy.

One can find in these statements all three of the basic elements of functionalism, and it is important to identify them because they often appear in isolation or in odd combination and confuse our understanding of the iconoclasts as much as they confused their aims.

The first is nineteenth-century rationalism, the child of the seventeenth-century Enlightenment, expressed in the pragmatic simplicities of the engineers and in the political simplicities of Gladstonian liberalism. It is often forgotten that rationalism was the cornerstone of the French academic tradition as codified by Guadet and Choisy, which had consistently taught for over a century that 'architecture needs more reasoning than inspiration'.*

* J.A.Borgnis (1823).

38

The failure of architects brought up in this tradition to appreciate what the engineers were doing was due not to hostility or jealousy but to the nowadays familiar difficulty that these people (while acknowledged to be equally versed in scientific method) were working in what was genuinely thought to be another discipline.

The second was the search for a new style, a familiar obsession of the Victorians, which the iconoclasts believed that history had proved would best be developed not by rummaging in the wardrobes of the past, nor by dredging an *art nouveau* out of the subconscious, but by allowing what T.G. Jackson called 'the suggestions of construction' to have their say – easier said, as all these pundits admitted, than done.

The third, and in the long run the most profound, was a conscientious investigation and embodiment of human needs, a care for *all* the parameters, and this is what Viollet meant when he so boldly, and so long before his time, spoke of 'the physical and moral requirements we have to satisfy' – incidentally in that one word setting the rather high moral tone which was to become an irritating trait of all the functionalists.

After the refreshing intuitions of Viollet-le-Duc it is salutary to take up Ruskin's Lamp of Truth (written, it is true, fourteen years earlier). For a moment, when Ruskin foresees 'a new system of architectural laws ... adapted entirely to metallic construction', or bids us 'leave your walls as bare as a planed board, or build them of baked mud and chopped straw if need be, but do not roughcast them with falsehood', or proposes that 'that building will generally be the noblest which to an intelligent eye discovers the great secrets of its structure', correspondences seem to exist. But then those cramping 'niceties of conscience' (his words) supervene, the pessimism overlays the optimism and one knows one has entered the haunted and guilt-ridden regions of the Victorian subconscious, which were to take England out of the race to create a new architecture for nearly a century. With this arch-imagist it is so often a matter of 'thou shalt not', and one is reminded of Gladstone's agonising self-examinations, except that his was a fundamentally sane nature. Two years after the publication of the

Seven Lamps, Paxton built the Crystal Palace, and the alternative Victorian tradition dramatically asserted itself.

This alternative tradition, vividly exemplified in the contrast between Scott's hotel and Barlow's train shed at St Pancras, has often been referred to as functionalist because it was empirical. Faced with a demand for new kinds of building, Victorian designers were forced to forget the copybooks and use their common sense or even their imagination. The consequences could be very plain, powerful and beautiful structures, but no nineteenth-century architect after Viollet saw their significance for architectural theory. It was assumed by everybody, by Labrouste and Brunel and Bunning and Bogardus, that if they were to rank as architecture they must be properly dressed, just as you could tell a gentleman by his clothes. Undecorated, they rated as engineering, and a historian like Fergusson would firmly class them as part of the vernacular as opposed to the architectural tradition.

Even Lethaby, speaking well after the turn of the century, was too gentle and fairminded a person to use the accents of iconoclasm. Scientific method would take you a certain distance, but the rest was art. Thus:

I want pathetic beauty in the cottage and in the barn, the most exquisite order, freshness and efficiency in our town streets, the uttermost of costly majesty in the city's public palace, and still something beyond for our cathedrals, some expression of infinite aspiration. . . . We need first the natural, the obvious, and, if it will not offend to say so, the reasonable, so that to these, which might seem to be under our own control, may be added we know not how or what of gifts and graces. Thus we may hope to combine the two realities, the reality of natural necessity and common experience with the reality of the philosophers, which is the ideal, and so reconcile again Science with Art.*

This sort of writing, set up in Baskerville type on handmade paper in the year of Le Corbusier's Citrohan house, seems to disqualify Lethaby from inclusion among the moderns, even though in principle it merely puts into Georgian language Gropius' 'The aesthetic satisfaction of the human soul is just as important as the

* W.R. Lethaby, *Form in Civilisation* (1922).

material', and even though Lethaby undoubtedly did, with his anathemas on style-mongering and delight in bicycles, mean to entice, if not to shock, the English out of their ingle-nooks.

The shocks of course came from elsewhere, and the first man in Europe to administer them was the Viennese Adolf Loos, with his now famous essay *Ornament and Crime* of 1908. No gentleman's dress for him:

> The symphonies of Beethoven could never have been written by a man who had to wear velvet, silk and lace. Anyone today who goes around in a velvet coat is no artist.

A bad forecast, as it turned out. Loos saw ornament as something primitive and rather disgusting, which it was the mark of a high civilisation to outgrow, and would presumably have regarded Ledoux and Soane as the culmination of the process to date.* It is difficult for us, after half a century of the Design and Industries Association and a couple of decades of the Council of Industrial Design, to remember how thick a jungle ornament was and how naked ordinary people felt without it. As recently as the 1930s the thing was a live issue, 'superfluous ornament' was under puritanical attack like superfluous hair, and the central characteristic of 'functionalist' design was thought to be the absence of ornament. For all this Loos' polemics and practice were responsible. His uncouth box-like houses were the ancestors of the 'packing-cases' the neo-Georgians were to deride in the thirties. If we are to trace back the immaculate white wall and steel window of the International Style to any one source, it can only be to him.

To Frank Lloyd Wright, his near contemporary, he ought therefore to have ranked as Public Enemy No. 1. For Wright, like most of his generation, was in love with ornament, and the problem was not to kill it but to revive it in a form appropriate to the new century and to machine technology. It was a problem he never solved but never got out of his system, where it created contradictions which he concealed by the use of magic words like 'plastic' and 'organic'. Thus of Louis Sullivan:

* He is known to have so regarded Schinkel.

The magic word *plastic* was used by the Master in reference to his ornament and the room itself began to show the effects of this ideal.

Blake* takes this sentence, with the quotation that follows, as the key to a mental transference which Wright achieved from 'plastic' ornament to 'plastic' structure.

Concrete is a plastic material. I saw a kind of weaving coming out of it. Why not weave a kind of building? Then I saw the shell. Shells with steel inlaid in them. . . . Lightness and strength! Steel the spider spinning a web within the cheap plastic material.†

And he goes on to describe continuity of stresses and the organic structures which this technique would eventually make possible.

There is no better example of the prophetic intuitions which were later to justify his claims to have thought of everything before anybody else. But his Usonian isolationism and his arrogant formalism alienated him from a movement whose main ethos was to be 'obedience to the programme'. The anti-European, anti-highbrow role which Wright assumed with such panache and which went down so well with his middle-Western apprentices probably concealed a deep sense of loneliness, but he was too magnificent an actor for it to be read except between the lines of his performance.

Wright specifically denied that he was an iconoclast, yet he belongs among them, was indeed the first of them, because of the splendid arrogance of his attack on the academies (for which he felt the same contempt as Viollet-le-Duc), on modernism as a rigid style, which he described as 'the 58th Variety', and on the *Ville Radieuse* which was itself, as he foresaw, headed for a new academicism. When the magnificent leonine figure lectured to London students on the eve of the Second World War‡ it was as if Wren had returned in his old age to slaughter the Burlingtonians and proclaim (in Wright's words) 'a new Declaration of

* Peter Blake, *The Master Builders* (1960).
† Frank Lloyd Wright, *An Organic Architecture* (1939).
‡ Frank Lloyd Wright, *An Organic Architecture* (1939).

Independence'. He was at the height of his powers (*Falling Water* and *Taliesin West* just built) and the sense of liberation was overwhelming:

Therefore the Declaration of Independence I bring you today is no mere negation. It is affirmative denial of the validity of any such thing as that servility on this earth and it is assertion of the right of life to live. In England you may proceed with the old traditional forms by which we were corrupted if you like. They are dead but more legitimate here; they are more or less yours, but they are not ours. I declare, the time is here for architecture to recognise its own nature, to realise the fact that it is out of life itself for life as it is now lived, a humane and therefore an intensely human thing.

We *know* that life is to be trusted. We *know* that the *interpretation* of life is the true function of the architect because we know that buildings are made for life, to be lived in and to be lived in happily.

Why then do you not trust life? Why does not great England on behalf of this great upward swing of life, on behalf of this desire to serve and interpret and develop humanity with fresh integrity, why does England not trust life?

You English listen, you approve, you say, 'Yes that is true', and you do nothing at all about it because a deep pessimism concerning life seems settling down among you if you don't watch out.

Here was a man who really did believe that we could shed the burdens of the past.

'Organic' architecture, the name which Wright appropriated for his escape route from our rigidities, was by then already an old story.* Wright had taken it over from Sullivan who had got it from Herbert Spencer, and in its narrower meaning (in so far as it had any meaning at all) it derived from biological evidences of the influence of function on form and vice versa, which some iconoclasts thought might be helpful in combating the Platonic ideal forms, deriving wholly from antique imagery and not from the parameters, which were the stock-in-trade of the academic tradition.

Yet in writing off this tradition Wright and his followers wholly

---

* In *Changing Ideals in Modern Architecture* (1965) Peter Collins claims that it was first so named in the Paris *Revue Générale d'Architecture* in 1863.

mistook its nature. It is no exaggeration to say that ever since the twelfth century the conventional wisdom of architecture had been rationality. Students were first taught the nature of materials, then construction, then ornament. Architecture was the art of *building*, it was building *plus*.* Whether the elements of building should be Doric or Vitruvian or pointed or abstract, whether the 'plus' should be Gothic or Renaissance was a secondary question and was scarcely discussed in French academic circles, however hotly it might be debated by English essayists. In this academic succession, which can be traced straight through the eighteenth and nineteenth centuries from Soufflot to Guadet, the classical language of architecture was taken for granted, and the main purpose of teaching was to convey that it must be used rationally and therefore economically and therefore elegantly. Just as the schoolboy who had mastered iambics was thought to be that much better equipped to write English verse, so the classically trained architect would be the best man to create a new architecture. Two sentences from Choisy will show how close the French academics came to the Wrightian philosophy:

The Greeks never visualised a building without the site that framed it and the other buildings that surrounded it . . . siting it as nature would have done. . . . The (Gothic) building becomes an organised being whose every part becomes a living member, its form formed not by traditional models, but by its function, and only its function.

Of course if Wright had read all this it might have reduced his head of steam: it is unnecessary and even harmful for iconoclasts to do a great deal of background reading.

For they correctly diagnosed the (to them) basic flaw in academic rationalism, which was that however logically it set forth the parameters it was still trafficking in imagery. Even Perret, who freed it from its cramping commitment to classical detail, and for this has his secure place among the iconoclasts, never got the Vitruvian armature out of his system, and survived into a changed world as the Mirabeau or the Kerensky of the revolutionary process.

* Thus Gropius (1935): 'So much for technique, but what about beauty?'

The fact is that before 1914 none of the leaders of the modern movement, with the strange but minor exception of Adolf Loos, had broken the bonds of imagery. These took three forms. There was the French classical academic tradition, the nursery not only of Perret but also of Le Corbusier, Gropius and Mies. There was the English craft tradition deriving from Morris and Mackintosh and evident in the attitudes of Lethaby, Berlage and Wright, as well as Gropius. And there was the Futurist manifesto, whose purpose was not to destroy imagery but to substitute new images for the old.

It was the War itself, in its devastating effect on men's minds, which precipitated this and so many other revolutions. If one takes three events of the years 1919–21 – the foundation of the Bauhaus, the definitive statement by J. J. P. Oud of the philosophy of the Dutch *de Stijl* group, and the appearance in Paris of Le Corbusier's magazine *L'Esprit Nouveau*★ – one finds in them all a clear and systematic radicalism quite different from the more confused or more hysterical utterances of the 1900s. The watershed of the War seemed to have disposed of the past, both as tutor and as enemy, and it seemed possible in those few years to make a genuine beginning. One can find in these three, Gropius, Oud and Le Corbusier, the whole of the theoretical basis of what came to be known as the International Style.

'Style' of course was the last word the iconoclasts used or wanted used of them. Thus Gropius:

We did not base our teaching on any preconceived ideas of form, but sought the vital spark of life behind life's ever-changing forms. . . . A 'Bauhaus Style' would have been a confession of failure and a return to that very stagnation and devitalising inertia which I had called it into being to combat.†

The Bauhaus method is now familiar. First, unlearn all second-hand ways of seeing and recapture the child's vision; then learn like a child to manipulate materials, shapes, colours, volumes; then

★ The three founders were Le Corbusier, the painter Ozenfant and the poet Paul Dermée.

† Walter Gropius, *The New Architecture and the Bauhaus* (1935).

learn to solve design problems of systematically increasing complexity; then get inside the factory and learn its methodology; finally design for industry. Gropius reached this system from William Morris beginnings and the Bauhaus gave more time to craftsmanship and 'learning by doing' than we can now afford or believe in. But its visual discoveries were real discoveries and its contempt for modish authority, whether dead or alive, is something the schools have never managed before or since. That it did all the same end up with a 'style' in no way diminishes its genuine radicalism. It was a style with roots.

Both in Gropius and in Oud we find Wrightian notions such as 'organic' architecture and the free flow of space virtually paraphrased. Oud sees the design of buildings and other industrial products and simple artefacts as emerging neither from past models (which are irrelevant) nor from considerations of utility (which are inadequate) but 'as if by themselves', embodying what Worringer in writing of medieval architecture was later to describe as the 'will to form' of an epoch – a concept now philosophically unfashionable but at least original in its day: it would certainly have raised eyebrows in the academies. Gropius and Oud add this other new conception of their age, 'Architecture is the mastery of space', which we have already seen graduating into the imagery of modernism in the work of Bauhaus teachers such as Klee and Moholy-Nagy. Here too we have Wright's favourite quotation from Lao-Tze, 'the reality of the building consists not of the walls but of the space within'. We are on that borderline where a new capability emerging naturally from the parameters is so exciting that it becomes elevated into an end itself. This is one of several meanings one could attach to Mies's well-known words – typical of his lapidary but ambiguous style – 'Wherever technology reaches its real fulfilment, it transcends into architecture'. It is a phenomenon we shall be returning to.

Le Corbusier is of course its most celebrated exponent. In his early days with Ozenfant and Dermée he sets up a Darwinian 'Law of Mechanical Selection', which 'establishes that objects tend towards a type that is determined by the evolution of forms, between

46

the ideal of maximum utility and the satisfaction of the necessities of economical manufacture, which conform inevitably to the laws of nature'. This is functionalism in its purest form, and is more uncompromising than either Wright or Oud or Gropius or Mies, with their concept of 'technology plus', were ever prepared to be. Hence the idealisation of aircraft, Atlantic liners, motorcars, silos or other engineering structures, which in 1919–21 were all at the post-primitive but pre-mannerist phase which we have earlier described as the classic moment.

It could have seemed at that moment that these artefacts had, 'as if by themselves', reached a finality of form like that of certain simple hand tools and utensils; and it may not have seemed utterly fanciful to link their principle of growth and form on the one hand with nature's organic processes and on the other hand with architecture. But before long Le Corbusier had moved from organic to mechanical analogies and was idealising the engineers, who 'overwhelm with their calculations our expiring architecture'. Finally, like Mies and Gropius, he was writing:

Architecture goes beyond utilitarian needs. You employ stone, wood and concrete, and with these materials you build houses and palaces. That is construction. Ingenuity is at work. But suddenly you touch my heart, you do me good, I am happy and I say 'This is beautiful'. That is Architecture. Art enters in.

This is almost exactly what Lethaby had been saying before the War.

So what did this exceptionally loquacious generation finally say? It amounted to this: that the aim of architecture, which is to make life more worth living, was the same as ever, but that the old methods had lost the power to do this; that the causes of this loss of power were to be found partly in the academic tradition with its insistence on inorganic symmetrical planning and antique imagery, partly in bourgeois addiction to 'motheaten boudoirs' and blindness to the beauties of the machine age, so that *its* imagery was obsolete too, partly in a building industry whose technology was still medieval, or not even that because of its failure to apply the lessons of medieval construction to the new

47

materials; and that the remedies were to unlearn all academic instruction, to play with shapes and textures and colours like a child in nursery school, to apply these new intuitions to the design of buildings as innocently and as radically as engineers apply mathematics to the design of machines, and above all to absorb the spirit of the new age, with its new materials, its new sense of space, its relaxed morality and egalitarianism of which mass production must be the technological expression.

The iconoclasts expressed these ideas in a small number of minor buildings, a minute fraction of the built environment, which were sufficiently revolutionary and sufficiently consistent to make their point. These buildings were white, to symbolise the rejection of ornament, they were asymmetrical to symbolise the rejection of the academies, they used steel or concrete columns instead of walls and black-painted steel windows instead of wooden ones to symbolise technology, they had flat roofs to symbolise the love of sun and rejection of rain and open plans to symbolise relaxed morality, egalitarianism and the new sense of space. Most of them were houses for intellectuals because they were the only patrons the iconoclasts could get, and compared with the houses of earlier generations they have suffered exceptionally from decay and mutilation, perhaps for two reasons. First, they were very masculine, even in the case of Le Corbusier to the point of brutality in detailing or lack of it, because the movement was itself overwhelmingly masculine in its futurism, austerity and idealisation of the machine: only a certain rare kind of woman could live with them. Second, they carried too high an emotional charge for a small house, which historically or normally is an unpretentious, relaxed, alterable structure, not designed by a great architect for purposes of propaganda, and survives for those reasons. It was like having a Masaccio over the living room fireplace or Beethoven to lunch. With the great name you bought inflexibility and subjection to the personality of the architect: a Barcelona chair was as unthinkable in a Wrightian house as a spaniel in a Miesian.

The masterpieces of the International Style were, as has been said, symbols, and of course they were a most rigid and mandatory Style, already so named by American connoisseurs like Barr, Hitchcock and Philip Johnson in the late 1920s. To these observers it seemed that the essential object of the whole operation had now been achieved. 'We have, as the Egyptians had or the Chinese, as the Greeks and our own ancestors in the Middle Ages before us, a Style. . . .'*

This had not of course been the object at all. What went wrong? It is the question asked of all revolutionaries when their call for freedom hardens into a new orthodoxy.

That the iconoclasts created a style that was loaded with symbolism and is now a powerful image is not the objection. For one thing, they were none of them in the last analysis functionalists, even in the sense in which they used the word. Art, they recognised, must enter in, and their iconoclasm consisted not in wishing to eliminate the aesthetic element but in scrapping all the useful tips and time-hallowed usages by which ordinary architects had been helped to master it. For another, they knew intuitively even if they did not say publicly that the situation was one in which an image was necessary to their revolution as indeed to all others. Their public attitude might be that man could live by bread alone but it was a very beautiful and healthful wholemeal loaf. What went wrong was that they ditched functionalism, and restricted their iconoclasm, prematurely and without even giving it a chance. There was nothing in their functionalism about human needs, let alone wants, no systematic investigation or indeed communication with the building and component industries, no thought of economics, no follow-up of the Futurists' intuition about the buy-and-scrap society we were moving into. They created images like armaments, and proved them superbly effective weapons of war, but they paid no attention to the parameters. Consequently their images, as they ought to have anticipated, proved expendable, and they left the idea of functionalism lying around on the battlefield for another generation to pick up and get to work on.

* Philip Johnson, *The International Style* (1930).

49

Again, it took a war to clear our minds – not this time, for the western nations, an apocalyptic drama but a war that seemed to have been won by patience and ingenuity. Here is David Medd, later of the Hertfordshire School team:

> We were part of a very small unit, whose personnel were directly involved with War Office policy, designing devices to serve the policy, making and testing prototypes, arranging for their production, training personnel in their use and gaining experience of their use in the field, from which new policies, designs and so on emerged. One had in this microcosmic form the whole design process and responsibility, and from it one realised that the architect in his normal practice position cannot do his job properly because he is only connected with a fragment of the process. Therefore one sought a work situation where the architect could be part of an organisation in which he could be employed with those conducting policy, in which he could be 'on the same side of the fence' as his clients, and in which he had the order book in his pocket to give him initiative and control of design.*

This records the faint origins of the first revolution in the *modus operandi* of the architect since he had come into existence as an identifiable professional in the Renaissance. The new men combined socialism in the Morris-Lethaby tradition with a natural and unemotional assimilation of the mature Bauhaus philosophy. Coolness and anonymity were the pride of their generation, and they spoke of the masterpieces of the pioneers as 'Capital A Architecture'. The words were Stirrat Johnson-Marshall's, to whom, with John Newsom of Hertfordshire, the initiation of the new English movement was largely due.

The essence of their revolution was the removal of that capital letter – of all capital letters, of Functionalism, Futurism, the Machine Aesthetic and the International Style, among others. In their place was to be a process, not an achievement, a process to which they gave the characteristically unemotive word *development*. But there was nothing imprecise about it. Development must be three-cornered: human needs, technical power and policy.

Human needs were to be assimilated not by receiving a 'client's

* David Medd, in a letter to the author (1969).

brief' like any barrister's clerk, but by 'finding out who to talk to, tracking down wisdom in other words; and the key that the architect alone possesses is imagination in realising the design implications of the wisdom he has tracked down'.* It was of course the great strength of the Hertfordshire set-up, later translated by Johnson-Marshall to government level, that client and architect worked side by side in one organisation, but it was the faith of the movement that this relation could be built up in ordinary non-official work, and that the young architects who had sat day after day as observers at the back of school classes would one day (as they did) do the same thing in factories, offices and universities. Scientific method – intuition tested by experiment – was wherever possible deployed to save their time, and it too given its head as a parameter.

It was largely as a result of this work (of the Building Research Station) that architects were introduced to the then rather novel idea that the size of windows might be influenced less by architectural conceptions of a desirable balance between solid and void, than by how much daylight was required in the room.†

This open-eyed attention to reality could not have developed into architecture at any affordable cost without the second weapon in the armoury: technical power. The right windows, the right components of any kind, simply did not exist in the industry, and to get them at the right price the architects had to do two things: design them alongside the manufacturers as Gropius had taught but hardly ever done, and order them in sufficient numbers and to a reliable production schedule far enough into the future. It was a basic tenet that by his control of the order-book the designer ensured that society got consumer-oriented and not producer-oriented buildings. The rest was a question of quantity, and it was the search for economies of scale in an increasingly competitive and industrialised industry which expanded the £$\frac{1}{2}$ million Hertfordshire programme of 1947 to the £20 million CLASP

* David Medd.

† Guy Oddie, 'The New English Humanism', *Architectural Review* (September 1963).

programme of 1967, and which later led to the long effort to find a system of dimensional co-ordination derived from human and technical parameters and not (like the Modulor) from imagery.

The third weapon was perhaps, in the light of the recent past, the most revolutionary of all: the architect's disappearance into an anonymous group of professional people. The word 'teamwork', which was later to become a substitute for thought, had, again, a precise meaning, involving an enhancement as well as a sacrifice of status. The architect abandoned the privilege of isolation while he produced his work of art, but took a seat at the table where final decisions were taken. At this table no take-it-or-leave-it solution would be unveiled. The process of development included ever deeper enquiry into human need (the educationalist's contribution), new techniques of cost analysis and cost control (the quantity surveyor's contribution), more and more refined design, and finally what came to be called 'feedback' – its continuous modification in the light of experience.

Thus architecture, which all through history had been a 'mystery', offered by a person working within a set of artistic rules he learnt as an apprentice or alternatively relying on his own sensibilities, then priced by the market, then built (if it did not have to be 'spoilt' to get the price down) by a lower caste not privy to the 'reason why', was to change its nature. It was to 'grow' on the drawing-board within the absolute disciplines of human need, site and climate, economics and technics, and no aesthetic preconceptions of any kind were to distort this growth. It seemed that the iconoclasts had won through at last. As the 'G' group had prophetically declared in the Berlin of the 1920s:

We refuse to recognise problems of form: we recognise only problems of building.

We must note that there were two different sides to this philosophy. One was humanist, the other technical. They worked together, but they were not indispensable to one another. The humane concern for the parameters did not *need* prefabrication for its fulfilment, and prefabrication *could* operate in a moral vacuum, as an end in itself. For example in a seller's market for housing, particularly after a war, mere quantity could override all other parameters, particularly in a politician's assessment. And whereas you could not run whole schools off assembly lines like motorcars, you could run whole houses, and did. There was the prospect of a million identical concrete or plastic boxes carpeting the landscape or stacked in the sky, and however assiduous the tree-planting or intricate the stacking system, it did not seem that either could ever cater for the fundamental human need to express oneself in one's habitat.

Architects were soon alerted to the risk of this, and a war developed between the politicians and the big contractors on the one hand, who had invested or wished to invest reputation or money in repetitive structures, and architects and component manufacturers on the other, who for aesthetic or business reasons were convinced that kits-of-parts which preserved flexibility of design were essential. Both were fond of quoting the Georgian terrace house as precedent, because you could call it either a repetitive structure or an assembly of standard components. In fact in the exact modern sense it was neither, for it was precisely its minor variations which made it tolerable and the disappearance of these in the nineteenth century which made the bye-law street intolerable. In this war the architect, provided he argued from all the parameters and not from some image he happened to be attached to, was bound to be more nearly right than the others, who clearly did not.

But did he so argue? In recent years it has become fashionable to doubt it. For one thing, the architect's pet method of prefabrication – a Meccano-type set of metal sections or a kit of concrete sticks and panels – was very much a part of the Mondrian-Miesian imagery and was therefore by no means aesthetically neutral. And it *needed* the architect for its imaginative assembly, so he was scarcely neutral either. Moreover there was a newly discovered chink in the architect's armour. The more devotedly he applied himself to the exact and economical tailoring of his building to the needs of the present the less adaptable was it likely to be to the

53

needs of the future. It was noticed that the generous spaces of Victorian buildings like railway stations obsolesced much less rapidly than the functionally detailed complexes of modern buildings like airports. In other words, there was a parameter missing, the parameter of growth and change; and to satisfy this, it could be right to throw overboard all that hard thinking. The advantages of the 'loose fit' were rediscovered.

The first statement of what he called the 'Principle of Indeterminacy' was made by the English architect John Weeks in 1964,* and like so much creative thinking it derived from a study of history. As a hospital architect, Weeks was well aware of 'the problem of sheltering an organisation which has a rate of growth and change which is so great that it makes its buildings obsolescent before they decay naturally'. He noticed that a century earlier Paxton had solved this problem in one way, by building the great glass tent of the Crystal Palace – a loose fit if ever there was one, and Brunel in another, by shipping out to the Dardanelles a prefabricated hospital consisting of pavilions clipped to a spine corridor which could be infinitely extended. The result was a new version of the functionalist philosophy:

I see no absolute value in shape control by sets of formal conventions. I am prepared to take the deformations of the site, the contractor's available techniques, the poverty of the clients and the principle of indeterminacy itself as shape-making forces and to derive systems which will allow them to operate as shape-makers. I see no more value in one force than in another. Nor can I see that to aim at completeness in an indeterminate situation is to aim high. It is simply to aim badly.

In a later paper Weeks takes the 'loose fit' idea further:

Too much information too early in the design process may clog the design machine.

and

My thesis is that by consideration of planning in terms of a much cruder relation between work done and the space necessary to house it,

* See J. Weeks, 'Hospitals for the 1970s', *RIBA Journal* (December 1964); and 'Indeterminate Architecture', *Transactions of the Bartlett Society*, Vol. II (1963–4).

not only can the planning process be speeded but the accommodation provided – being less accurately tailored to specific pieces of work – will retain its viability longer.*

At first glance this could be interpreted as a reaction to formalism, to the take-it-or-leave-it work of art. The opposite is the case. Weeks has abandoned formalism in abandoning the finite design concept and going for indeterminacy. Far from dusting up architecture and restoring it to its pedestal, the argument has been said to amount to the end of architecture.

The elevations have not been altered in any way since they came from the engineer's office. Each elevation was a surprise and delight to us.

With this last addition, the lore of functionalism seems complete – and it has to be complete to be meaningful. Devotion to human need in the absence of technological mastery is ineffective; productive genius blind to wants and needs is brutal; absorption in the contemporary problem with no eye to the accelerating pace of cultural change is stupid. But if all the parameters are present and given their full authority, then undoubtedly the process of design can take the form of a computer programme.

This emotive conclusion hoists of course in all our minds a danger signal, and it is not a hypothetical *reductio ad absurdum*. Ironically, the most complete and conspicuous examples of this design process are not the high-minded socially-oriented buildings in which it originated, but the speculative office blocks in our cities in which it now operates on a far more dramatic scale. With the planner supplying the plot ratio, the developer the economics, the potential user the precise standard of catalogue curtain-wall and climate-control the situation can justify, and the certainty of new management techniques within the lifetime of the building the flexibility, the urban environment, complete with indeterminacy, is predetermined. And the system begins to work backwards into the schools, where teaching techniques are bound to

* J. Weeks, 'Design for Growth and Change and the Project Team Concept', *The Canadian Hospital* (November 1967).

change just as rapidly. The Hertfordshire old guard protests:

The only flexibility you have is the ability to change the relative areas of adjacent spaces. . . . You are in danger of having uniformity of character throughout. With your ubiquitous steel-faced partitions . . . you have brought perpetual poverty for the present for the price of flexibility in the future. . . .*

Alongside this almost plaintive protest from the generation that grew up in the 1930s, a counterblast from an entirely new quarter began to make itself felt in the mid-60s. This was the iconoclasm of the American New Left, and it took the form of a radical attack on mainstream Modern Architecture as it had become codified in the impeccable commercial architecture derived from Mies. The anti-academic tone was traditionally Usonian and reminiscent of Wright's own Declaration of Independence. The novelty lay in the content, which was deliberately anti-modern in its appeal to historical precedent. It was also provocatively and shamelessly Mannerist. Thus Robert Venturi:

Architects can no longer afford to be intimidated by the puritanically moral language of orthodox Modern architecture. I like elements which are hybrid rather than 'pure', compromising rather than 'clean', distorted rather than 'straightforward', ambiguous rather than 'articulated', perverse as well as impersonal, boring as well as 'interesting', conventional rather than 'designed', accommodating rather than excluding, redundant rather than simple, vestigial as well as innovating, inconsistent and equivocal rather than direct and clear. I am for messy vitality over obvious unity. I include the non sequitur and proclaim the duality.†

Venturi's view is that the childishly simple list of parameters given in chapter 1 and finally adopted as programmatic in the 1950s grossly oversimplifies the subtleties of human needs.

The growing complexities of our functional problems must be acknowledged. I refer, of course to those programs, unique in our time,

* David Medd, 'People in Schools: an Attitude to Design', *RIBA Journal* (June 1968).
    † Robert Venturi, *Complexity and Contradiction in Architecture* (1966).

56

which are complex because of their scope, such as research laboratories, hospitals, and particularly the enormous projects at the scale of city and regional planning. But even the house, simple in scope, is complex in purpose if the ambiguities of contemporary experience are expressed. This contrast between the means and the goals of a program is significant. Although the means involved in the program of a rocket to get to the moon, for instance, are almost infinitely complex, the goal is simple and contains few contradictions; although the means involved in the program and structure of buildings are far simpler and less sophisticated technologically than almost any engineering project, the purpose is more complex and often inherently ambiguous.

What applies to the building applies *a fortiori* to the city.

Architects and planners who peevishly denounce the conventional townscape for its vulgarity or banality promote elaborate methods for abolishing or disguising honky-tonk elements in the existing landscape, or for excluding them from the vocabulary of their new townscapes. But they largely fail either to enhance or to provide a substitute for the existing scene because they attempt the impossible. By attempting too much they flaunt their impotence and risk their continuing as supposed experts.

On both sides, this controversy reverberates far beyond the bounds of the individual building. We are in the field of contemporary macro-aesthetics, to which we must now turn our attention.

4

Macro-aesthetics

All through history architects have included in their role the design of cities, not only for the sufficient reason that you never could draw a line between the design of a building and the design of a group, but also because planning ideal town shapes was a *divertissement*, a kind of spare-time geometrical patience, and an escape from clients. It would be tedious to work through examples, which occur from Vitruvius through to Brasilia and were particularly numerous in the early Renaissance, when they attracted pattern-fanciers in the same mode as the garden-conceits of the same period. It was a craft as innocent, and as devoid of three-dimensional significance, as embroidery.

Meanwhile, like the creatures of a coral reef, the vernacular builders went on with their subtle, pragmatic, for long periods scarcely perceptible emendation of the urban fabric, a process of cell renewal purposive and aesthetically motivated in varying degrees, but inevitably limited in scope. It was not until the Baroque, as we have seen, that abstract and concrete, geometry and visual experience, were brought together on a scale capable of penetrating the whole city and later the landscape matrix itself. Macro-aesthetics begin here. If the scale of the operation is ever to achieve a significance beyond mere extensiveness, we shall find in the seventeenth and eighteenth centuries the first models and warnings.

To Lewis Mumford,* Pope Sixtus v was the first bulldozer, and

* Lewis Mumford, *The City in History* (1961).

he rightly denounces this all too easy destruction of the organic growth of centuries, of the raw material of human lives. Yet he goes on to quote Daniel Burnham's famous observation: 'Make no little plans, for they have no power to stir men's minds.' This is our dilemma when we think about the great fire-breaks of the Baroque. Before this final solution established itself all over the world, Venice existed, Oxford existed, Amsterdam and Berne and Siena existed – no mean urban scrub but supreme human creations exhibiting kinds of urban order that could well be more sophisticated as well as more mysterious than any that were to succeed them. It was Mumford's theory that the medieval town went down before the new geometry because 'the sealed urban container proved the impossibility of meeting the situation by local adjustments directed towards self-sufficiency, as the National States of our own day, however large, must likewise discover'. But Oxford and Amsterdam leapt their walls and moats with ease and without sacrificing their principles of growth, the one quadrangular, the other annular; and both cities developed a relationship with the matrix in which they were set – the one in green fields, the other in green water – which welcomed and embraced it among buildings and never shut it out. Most spectacular of all, Venice used one material for wall and highway and could have gone on island-hopping for ever.

So it was surely no deficiency in old ways of building cities that led to the Baroque triumph, but the force of the idea itself. Sixtus v mastered and displayed the geography of Rome in the same way that a surveyor maps a wild landscape, using conspicuous monuments as landmarks and obelisks as trig points. Intervisibility by shrinking distances and establishing relationships makes the scene comprehensible as far as the horizon. A whole city achieves the identity and meaning which previously could only be found in a small town or the centre of a large one. This was something much more powerful than the standard colonial gridiron with its identical streets ending in sky: here some familiar object crowned each vista, if necessary rebuilt or re-fronted on an appropriate scale, and when you finally reached it you could admire the architect's ingenuity in bringing all the converging streets into a symmetrical *place*, itself appropriately scaled to set off its commanding monument. This wresting of order out of chaos was the test of skill that separated the men from the boys.

At one end of this range of skill is the group of squares at Nancy, the most refined sequence of outdoor drawing-rooms in Europe; at the other, every *rond-point* or *Place de la Republique* in Latin American or French colonial towns, with trousered or gesticulating bronze centre-piece, segments of lobelias and dusty cannas, and circle of impoverished palms. Somewhere in between lie garden cities like Welwyn and New Delhi, Griffin's Canberra – a brave effort to apply the Sistine doctrine – and L'Enfant's Washington – a distillation of the lessons of Paris and Versailles. Paris itself is of course the central case-book, where the academic tradition displays its whole range of grandeurs and banalities.

Like all really successful ideas, it was depreciated by endless repetition and by misuse by second-class minds. But it had flaws of its own, on top of the moral one of brutality already referred to. It ignored contours, although it sometimes received bonuses from them in the form of surprises it had done nothing to deserve. It was extraordinarily unsubtle, with its predictable feature at the end of every avenue and its absurdly limited visual repertoire. It never solved the simple dilemma created by its elementary geometry, between right-angles which made no provision for diagonal journeys and diagonals which produced misshapen building plots.

Most significantly for the future, it set up for the first time a two-class urban environment. The first-class patron only saw the scene from the auditorium and could admire the elegance and even the grandeur of the sets. The second-class lived among the pipe-runs and the dusty props off-stage. Haussmann's handsome network of tree-lined boulevards condemned Paris to a criss-cross of multi-purpose roads which cut through the grain of its historic texture and would eventually make it the hardest city in the world to restructure. We are fortunate in the persistent failure to clamp this discipline on to London, starting with Wren and not ending until the Royal Academy's wartime fantasies of the 1940s.

In between these alien exercises, the English realised a variant of their own, and their first original contribution to town planning. Its inventors were the Woods of Bath in the first half of the eighteenth century, and its special features were the escape from axiality, the introduction of the curved terrace, and a characteristically piecemeal and pragmatic approach, piece added to piece as freely as in a game of dominoes. Complementary to this relaxation of the academic formula was its setting in picturesque instead of formal landscape – a domestication of the Versailles idea which amounted to total transformation, and opened the way to the great age of British estate development. But neither the Woods in Bath nor Nash in London saw beyond the stage-set. One's stroll up Gay Street or down Regent Street was enlivened by handsome skin-deep Roman architecture and the backs never entered the architect's mind. In the end these showpieces turned out less functional and so less meaningful for town living than the ordinary residential streets and squares of the three British capitals, just as overseas the simple Vitruvian layouts of small cities like Savannah, Georgia and Adelaide, South Australia, expressing more egalitarian philosophies, made better long-term sense than the vast vistas the whole world aspired to imitate from the Paris of Louis XIV and Napoleon.

If we stand back and picture the European scene as it was in the early nineteenth century – and there is no need to look outside Europe since it was still the copybook of the world – what relevance has it for us in our incredibly different age? Away from the ravaged and ecologically unique Mediterranean littoral, most of pre-railway Europe still wore its millennial aspect as a forested region interspersed with cleared areas of all sizes laid out in a more or less regular agricultural patchwork. Straight lines of Roman roads and canals and strip cultivation predominated, and at intersections or river crossings clustered starfish market towns, some ringed by fortification. No flyer could have supposed it anything but a man-shaped landscape, but the man was a surveyor or engineer, and no aesthete.

Then in the Ile de France and the south of England there is a change. In France the straight lines form equal angles about specific centres, meet one another at symmetrical junctions and create over the whole landscape an elaborate system of regular triangulation which indiscriminately knits towns and country. Just as in Baroque Rome a single formal hierarchy controls interior and exterior space, so that the church and its piazza are part of a single plan, so in Bourbon France *château* and forecourt and stables and village and avenue and forest ride are all one system, horizon-wide. England absolutely lacks this. The landscape, a century and a half after John Evelyn and half a century after Capability Brown, is maturely 'picturesque': brakes and coverts and woodlands and arable and pasture are all free-form, and this organic pattern is softened still further by a million hedgerow trees. Small segments and squares of this material penetrate the towns, but the streets and rows of houses are laid out on another principle, cellular, repetitive and rectangular.

Almost subconsciously the two countries seem to have developed landscapes which suited their political and demographic futures. Thinly populated and centralised, France went for a unified and comprehensible structure within which the human eye and mind could command great distances, while England developed a diverse and locally oriented tangle in which larger numbers could be tucked away. Thus both have their contemporary relevance.

Pre-industrial Europe left us three universally valid, often neglected legacies. First, these beginnings of a visual link-up between townscape and landscape. We have seen how the medieval image of the city drew its power from the contrast between the two, how the introverted town stood on the defensive against a hostile or at best a servile landscape, how the walled garden reflected this, defying with its elaborate geometrical patterns the raw dullness of external nature. We have seen the universal men of the Renaissance from Alberti to Leonardo first discovering then systematising the universal habitat. The breakthrough from the town into the country and vice versa were part of this process. The urban shaft of space penetrated to the horizon at the same moment as the asterisk of forest rides centred on the hunting lodge became a main theme of town planning. Simultaneously in England William Kent 'leapt the fence and saw that all nature was a garden', domesticating the landscape at the same moment as nature was for the first time given its formal *entrée* to the public spaces of the town.

Important as all this was, it all happened in the realm of pure, indeed rather precious, aesthetics. That the working landscape might have its own formal language derived from its own functional necessities was as inconceivable to Le Notre or Kent or anybody in the landscape movement as was functionalism of any kind to the architects of their age. Even the sensible and practical-minded Humphrey Repton could advise the placing of a herd of cattle in a certain field to give a sense of distance and the retention of an unwanted cottage so that its smoke might animate the scene.

This is not however the whole story, and we may take Repton, whose career and attitudes bridge the eighteenth and nineteenth centuries, as the representative of the second of the three 'futurible' legacies of the pre-industrial age.

I have discovered that utility must often take the lead of beauty, and convenience be preferred to picturesque effect, in the neighbourhood of man's habitation.*

Repton was a true eclectic, capable of going all the way, as with his cows and smoke, with the most implacable exponents of the picturesque, yet capable of writing in 1816 of the 'old magnificent taste for straight lines'. Universal solutions, either of the Le Notre or the Brown persuasion, were to him fatal and impoverishing short-cuts, and it was his eye for the parameters which links him with our own age. In him the landscape movement demonstrated its flexibility and ability to compromise, but with him also it began its descent into Victorian bittiness and triviality. As for 'utility', Repton sees it as the converse of beauty and never as a form-giver in its own right.

The farm . . . is for ever changing the colour of its surface in motley

* H.Repton, *Sketches and Hints on Landscape Gardening* (1794).

and discordant hues. It is subdivided by straight lines of fences. The trees can only be ranged in formal rows along the hedges; and there the farmer claims a right to cut, prune and disfigure.*

Like the boulevard planner, Repton sweeps this little real-life problem under the carpet.

Third and most potent legacy of his age is the terrace house. Anglo-Saxon architects of this century have used the traditional terrace as their main evidence in combating sentimental notions popularly attributed to the garden city movement, to the exent of conferring on the terrace house a sentimentality of its own. Its origins were entirely realistic. In a nation of small towns seldom compressed by fortification requirements or population pressures townspeople had always lived side by side in houses, each with its front door to the street and its walled yard at the back. When in the eighteenth century the population at last did surge and the enclosures drove numbers of people into the towns, the rectangular, fire-resisting, space-saving brick box was the obvious way to house them. So what had previously been individual and diverse became standardised and mass-produced, and nobody fretted about it. Picturesque notions had not spread from landscape into architecture, despite the experiments of one or two highbrows like Horace Walpole, and towns were still severely Euclidean. Moreover the repetitive nature of the structure lent itself easily to the rhythms of Palladian architecture, so that the terrace could be dressed as a palace if need be. So the narrow-fronted London house, with storeys according to social standing, imposed itself, to the amusement of continentals. Summerson quotes a Frenchman of 1817:

These narrow houses, three or four storeys high – one for eating, one for sleeping, a third for company, a fourth underground for the kitchen, a fifth perhaps at top for servants – and the agility, the ease, the quickness with which the individuals of the family run up and down and perch on the different levels, give the idea of a cage with its sticks and birds.†

* *Observations* (1803), quoted in N.Pevsner, *Humphrey Repton, a Florilegium* (1948).
† John Summerson, *Georgian London* (1945).

64

The terrace house had two immense social assets: its classlessness – or rather its social adaptability – and its backyard, where a family could do what it liked in the open air, on the real ground. It would always be hard to devise anything better.

We may sum up by noting that by the beginning of the nineteenth century Europe had seen the dawn of macro-aesthetics, the dawn of landscape functionalism and the dawn of a humane system of mass housing. We have to go on to note that the rest of the century, which was so prolific of new ideas in architecture, added no new ideas whatever in planning: it merely corrupted and brutalised those it inherited. The Baroque conquest of space ossified into the sterile formulae of *Beaux Arts* planning, the English working countryside lost its economic base with the repeal of the Corn Laws and decayed into sentimentality, and the terrace house symbolically lost its back garden, blacked its face, and turned into the back-to-back slum.

If we are to understand what followed, we must be clear about why this was so. At the root of the failure was the triple political/scientific/romantic revolution that we date for convenience from 1789. This destroyed authoritarian government, the eotechnic world and the Renaissance cosmos in one fell swoop, and although in France the Napoleonic counter-revolution established a synthetic and in some respects durable substitute, it had no cultural roots. 'Napoleon's dominion was like a July day in Egypt', wrote Ugo Foscolo, 'all clear, brilliant and blazing; but all silent; not a voice heard; the stillness of the grave.' Victorian Britain, lacking even this backbone, was totally and congenitally and wilfully incapable of synoptic vision. It dealt, as John Piper remarks of Romantic Art, with the particular.

Hence, one must suppose, the staggering Victorian blindness to *relationships*, which enabled builders to put up beefy red Flemish-style post offices in Cotswold villages and to turn a blind eye (in the bad fashion already set by John Nash) to the backs of their richly fronted clubs and hotels. Hence too the conviction that 'where there's muck there's money' – and not only money: the shining new invention secretly assembled in the junk-yard was and remains a potent British myth. Only in Germany, with its proud municipal traditions and its constellation of small-scale bureaucracies vying with one another in neatness and efficiency, was town-planning decently carried on through the nineteenth century, so that it proved strong enough to cope with the pressures of industrialisation when they hit the country later in the age.

There is no need here to re-tell how in Britain the population explosion and the ideology of Darwin and Samuel Smiles between them escalated into the Victorian nightmare, since this image is now secure in the mythology of the modern movement – our own Chaos and Old Night. But it is worth remarking that the Romantics (until the burden of guilt became intolerable) really *wanted* cities to be a confused undergrowth out of which the towers and spires of genius could rise like forest trees. Thus Wordsworth, at the very beginning of the century, was writing in *The Prelude*:

> As the black storm upon the mountain-top
> Sets off the sunbeam in the valley, so
> That huge fermenting mass of human-kind
> Serves as a solemn background, or relief,
> To single forms and objects, whence they draw,
> For feeling and contemplative regard,
> More than inherent liveliness and power.

Pugin's vision, which we can see miraculously enshrined in the silhouette of the Houses of Parliament, inspired all those smoky bird's eye views of Victorian Birmingham and reached a fulfilment he could never have dreamt of or approved in the spiky New York of the first-generation millionaires, now lost to us among the flat-tops both in America and England. Perhaps that home of lost causes, the City of Dreaming Spires – itself a typically Victorian description – will in the long run be its only surviving representative. Certainly if we are to regard this as the one Victorian contribution to macro-aesthetics, it was one that had no long-term relevance.

Yet it would be wrong to say good-bye so summarily to the visual world of the nineteenth century, a world uniquely rich and variegated because it filled the great anarchic chasm between the Rule of Taste and the Rule of Technology, between the Augustan and Electronic eras. The great cities it amassed in a kind of dream lay in landscapes more maturely beautiful than anything seen before or since, a golden world recorded for us by Samuel Palmer and Sisley, by Kilvert and Hardy, by Thoreau and Proust. Skiffs and sailboats on the silent lakes, ponies and traps outside the haberdashers in country towns, brightly polished new trains in brightly painted new stations, fields full of wildflowers, birdsong and butterflies, and alive with people walking the footpaths and riding the lanes – these are the images the writers and painters leave with us. It was a world of infinite variety. The American wilderness was the epic landscape of the Western sagas. The Zen gardens of Japan and the *Feng Shui* landscapes of China were undiscovered, the canals of Bangkok unpolluted, the shores of the Mediterranean unexploited except for Lord Brougham's first few villas at Cannes. Even the Indian economy was viable, for the planet and its population were a nice easy fit. Artefacts were made for long life and kept in trim, machines finished with pride and lovingly looked after. As for the cities, so much derided, they had their joys, if we set against the London of Dickens and Doré the Paris of the Impressionists. If the mainstream of architectural thought passes inescapably through the puritanical minds of Victorian social reformers, and we have to go with it, we must remember that the built environment which they rightly realised was in a state of decline sheltered a life which while brutal was not joyless. It was simply that its builders and its architects had no way forward to offer. So the role of Victorian town building was finally negative: it was to thicken up the compost heap from which the lilies of a new architecture would eventually grow; or as the reformers would have put it, to pile up the prison walls until the only hope was escape. 'As builders of splendid cities', Clough Williams-Ellis was to write in the 1930s, 'the British are more ignominious than rabbits'.

It was an English civil servant and a Scottish biologist who led the break-out, and significantly neither of them were architects:

the Victorian city had become a social problem. Ebenezer Howard, while he accepted the prevailing reformist view of the horrors of metropolitan life, was mainly activated by a desire to rehabilitate the depopulated and depressed countryside. 'Garden City' was something more than just another healthy utopia on the lines projected by earlier reformers: it was the source of an agricultural revival, exchanging manure for vegetables and manufactures for cottage industries. It was to settle into its 'estate' in a symbiosis totally different from the earlier image of the fortified town in the wilderness. 'Allotments, cow pastures, fruit farms, convalescent homes, farms for epileptics, children's cottage homes' – these were some of the busy activities Howard placed in his green belt.★ While nature penetrated the town, man was to penetrate the landscape.

Considering how diagrammatic and non-visual Howard's model was, it is remarkable how all its main proposals have survived, particularly at Welwyn. The central circular park with its ring of public buildings, the Grand Avenue 'four times as wide as Portland Place', with small houses peeping between the trees on either side, even the average house plot of 2,000 square feet, all were faithfully reproduced. Well into the 1950s, 'institutions and asylums' got automatic planning permission in green belts.

The only reject was his 'Crystal Palace' or circular glass-roofed shopping arcade, a mid-Victorian concept which unfortunately did not appeal to the neo-Georgian architects who translated Howard's ideas into bricks and mortar. Nor did the firm perimeter, though accepted in theory, hold in practice. The garden cities grew like any other town, and only now is the principle of growth by colonisation, producing in due course an urban cluster, coming into its own.

Howard's importance lay not only in the viability of his positive ideas, which firmly established the self-contained, publicly-owned, green-belted, medium-density, industrial satellite as the escape route from the metropolitan swamp, but also in the violence of

★ Ebenezer Howard, *Tomorrow: A Peaceful Path to Real Reform* (1898).

the negative reaction they provoked. The expression 'Garden City', misapplied to countless low-density speculative estates on the fringes of London and Paris, came in sophisticated circles to represent, in the words of a 1930s controversialist,* 'a hermaphrodite, sterile, imbecile, a monster; abhorrent and loathsome to the Nature which he worships'. The predictable stampede into metroland, led by the railway and accelerated by the motorcar, had provoked a counter-attack in which genuine alarm at landscape spoliation, genuine affection for the compact pre-industrial town, self-defence by an earlier wave of escapists and good old home-counties snobbery were powerfully combined. The result for urbanism was a much more affectionate study of towns as they were, which would eventually even embrace what was left of the grey areas from which the stampede had originated. The Forsytes, leaving Robin Hill swamped in suburbia, returned to live in Islington or Lambeth.

But long before that, a much more profound and penetrating study of urban anatomy had appeared. Patrick Geddes constructed no models. His mind was Edwardian rather than Victorian, and he rejected the amateurism which allowed the Victorians to suppose that a man could invent anything – even a town design. Encyclopaedic rather than pragmatic, his concern was with nothing less than the whole human habitat, which he examined with the eye of the historian as well as the ecologist. Historically, he was the first to grasp the central cultural position of technics, and to set forth the deliberately black-and-white contrast between the regressive palaeotechnic and the emergent neotechnic cultures which Mumford was to refine and expand into his massive *Technics and Civilisation*. And he was the first to write about cities as organisms rather than as works of art or inert assemblages of works of architecture. Geddes tore up the conventional maps in which towns were dots and political boundaries lines, and showed what was really there – swarming populations, resources, barriers, movement. The region was the body, the city its pulsating heart, or, in another metaphor, an opening flower:

* Thomas Sharp, *Town and Countryside* (1932).

Towns must now cease to spread like expanding ink-stains and grease-spots; once in true development, they will repeat the star-like opening of the flower, with green leaves set in alternation with ist golden rays.*

It was commonsense to Geddes, using the diagnostic method that came naturally to him, that the cure of cities must emerge from a meticulous and unprejudiced examination. Thereafter, 'conservative surgery' was what he liked to recommend, retaining all possible healthy tissue and restoring circulation by a few delicate touches rather than the great gashes and amputations favoured by engineers like Haussmann. Above all, dropping the medical analogy, he realised that planning is a process and not a product, with no beginning and no end, and that a permanent 'civic exhibition' was the way to communicate and involve people in this process.

The School of Civics, with its observatory and museum of survey . . . must become a familiar institution in every city, with its civic library in rapid growth and widening use, and all as a veritable power-house of civic thought and action.

Geddes dealt in understanding, not in power. Whereas Howard had devoted two-thirds of his book to economics and tactics, Geddes had no flair for either. *Cities in Evolution* is a scrappy masterpiece, esoteric in expression, penetrating the thought of a minority of intellectuals long before it entered the armoury of political action. Its first inadequate results were a group of hand-somely presented 'planning reports' for American or British cities or regions, most of which appeared in the late 1920s, a time when the central concern of individuals was making money or losing it, and which had no practical effect because governments neither understood economic planning nor possessed the powers to put it into effect.

Nowhere was the tragedy of *laissez-faire* exploitation more dramatically displayed than in the United States, an earthly para-dise more savagely and profitably despoiled than any other in the

* Patrick Geddes, *Cities in Evolution* (1915).

world. Henry James, returning after twenty years to stay with his brother in New England, wrote:

The land's all right. It seemed to plead, the pathetic presence, to be liked, to be loved, to be stayed with, lived with, handled with some kindness, shown even some courtesy of admiration.*

But Nature is not merely passive, as in this image of the neglected mother. It is also an avenging fury, and at the end of its deceptive patience has time and again risen up and destroyed civilisations which help themselves to one resource while squandering others. It used to be part of the South's contempt for the Yankees that they did precisely this and had no feeling for the land, but when the slump came it was not only the stock exchange which collapsed, but the topsoil in the Cornbelt and the Deep South. The 'synoptic' view of the unity of natural resources that had lain at the base of the teaching of Geddes and Mumford had proved beyond the capacity of businessman and farmer alike.

It had become a matter for the nation. In his message to Congress setting up the Tennessee Valley Authority in 1933, Roosevelt wrote:

It should be charged with the broadest duty of planning for the proper use, conservation and development of the natural resources of the Tennessee River basin and its adjoining territory for the general social and economic welfare of the nation . . . and be clothed with the necessary power to carry these plans into effect.

State boundaries significantly based on the abstraction of latitude and longitude were to be ignored and the resources of a river basin, its water and land and forests, were to be handled like a 'seamless web', of which you could not touch one strand without affecting another.

The power was at last there, but the great achievement of the TVA was in its diffusion, and in the patience and dedication with which the leaders involved the whole community in the enterprise. In this David Lilienthal was the prime mover, and he saw quite clearly what was at stake.

* Henry James, *The American Scene* (1904).

The physical achievements that science and technology now make possible *may bring no benefits*, may indeed be evil, unless they have a moral purpose, unless they are conceived and carried out for the benefit of the people themselves.

But such a moral purpose alone is not enough to insure that resource development will be a blessing and not a curse. Out of TVA experience in this valley I am persuaded that to make such a purpose effective two other principles are essential.

First, that resource development must be governed by the unity of nature herself.

Second, that the people must participate actively in that development.

The physical job is going to be done; of that I think we can be sure. But if, in the doing, the unity of nature's resources is disregarded, the price will be paid in exhausted land, butchered forests, polluted streams, and industrial ugliness. And, if the people are denied an active part in this great task, then they may be poor or they may be prosperous but they will not be free.*

The principle of the unity of nature's resources he expressed thus:

Water falls upon a mountain slope six thousand feet above the level of the river's mouth. It percolates through the roots and the sub-surface channels, flows in a thousand tiny veins, until it comes together in one stream, then in another, and at last reaches a TVA lake where it is stored behind a dam. Down a huge steel tube it falls, turning a water wheel. Here the water's energy is transformed into electricity, and then, moving onward toward the sea, it continues on its course, through ten such lakes, over ten such water wheels. Each time, electric energy is created. That electricity, carried perhaps two hundred miles in a flash of time, heats to incredible temperatures a furnace that transforms inert phosphate ore into a chemical of great possibilities. That phosphatic chemical, put upon his land by a farmer, stirs new life in the land, induces the growth of pastures that capture the inexhaustible power of the sun. Those pastures, born of the energy of phosphate and electricity, feed the energies of animals and men, hold the soil, free the streams of silt, man-made reservoirs, from which more electricity is generated as more water from the restored land flows on its endless course.

Such a cycle is restorative, not exhausting. It gives life as it sustains

* David Lilienthal, *TVA: Democracy on the March* (1944).

life. The principle of unity has been obeyed, the circle has been closed. The yield is not the old sad tale of spoliation and poverty, but that of nature and science and man in the bounty of harmony.

How arty and decadent seem the scruples of Humphrey Repton about the inelegancies of agriculture alongside the grand perspectives of what was still the American dream!

From five thousand feet the great change is unmistakable. There it is stretching out before your eyes, a moving and exciting picture. You can see the undulation of neatly terraced hillsides, newly contrived to make the beating rains 'walk, not run, to the nearest exit'; you can see the grey bulk of the dams, stout marks across the river now deep blue, no longer red and murky with its hoard of soil washed from the eroding land. You can see the barges with their double tows of goods to be unloaded at new river terminals. And marching towards every point on the horizon you can see the steel criss-cross of electric transmission towers.

And with Repton's concern about the farmer's unsentimental attitude to trees compare this:

One kind of tree is chosen to be grown for fence posts, another because its branches make good cotton spindles; the nuts of this one can be sold to the shelling plant near by; one species is chosen for use as wildlife food, another for its beauty or the shade it gives for the family in the farmyard, and for the fruit pods that fatten cattle and pigs. All the trees help to save the soil, hold the water on the land.

In the Tennessee Valley we saw the first region-wide application of what later came to be called the 'principle of multiple use'. The message was quickly picked up by English planners, conscious of the increasing strain on the land resources of their small island. By the end of the war we were thinking in terms like these:

The planner is the reverse of the one-idea man. If ideas were balls he would be the man who keeps eight or nine in the air at once. To do this his synchronisation must be so accurate as to partake of the nature of pattern, and the pattern will be the result of the way he combines the balls, so that there will be as many patterns as there are combinations. A new pattern does not demand new balls, only a new combination

73

of the old balls. Neither is it enough just to fling the important ones in the air and leave the rest in the basket. In a healthy society there is space and time for every activity, whatever the combination – the agent of multiple use being multiple need. To take only the mundane demands of work, entertainment, relaxation, shelter – no durable way of life on any workable chunk of land can be conceived without all these contacts dancing in the air together. The combination will vary as one or other takes precedence, and the landscape pattern will vary with it. Two things are reciprocal, the pattern and the combination.*

Thus in Britain at almost exactly the mid-century a tenable theory of functionalism, which admirably suited the national mood of the time – earnest, pragmatic and disillusioned – had by different routes emerged in almost identical statements in the field of building and in the field of landscape. The theory was tenable in the sense that it sounded sensible and had been proved workable in Hertfordshire and Tennessee. But it had, as we have seen, a fundamental flaw, which was that it took care of all the parameters except time. Just as the exact tailoring of the building to the needs of one moment made it that much less adaptable to growth and change, so the characteristic pattern produced by multiple use of a certain landscape in a certain generation left no elbow room for changes in farming, forestry, technology or resource development. Even while Lilienthal was writing his book in the 1940s, as indeed he knew but could not say, the atomic bomb was under development in the Valley – an ironical product of the New Deal idealism that had sent in the bulldozers.

In England the 'seamless web' of unified resource development ran into troubles of another kind. Here the landscape was neither virgin wilderness nor tragic victim of rape but 'the greatest contribution England has made to European arts'† – a reigning beauty in the full flower of maturity. Here from long experience of mines and railways it was clear to all that anything new was worse. The transmission towers that symbolised hope revived in the TVA were known as 'eyesores' in rural England, and the

---

* Lionel Brett, 'Attitudes to Landscape', *Architectural Review* (June 1949).
† Editorial in *Architectural Review* (September 1949).

plantations which gripped the topsoil and repelled erosion were lumped together as conifers and excited the special hatred and contempt of British aesthetes.

The point is – are we willing, under the duress of forceful economic argument, to forego what is left of the English agricultural park landscape and accept its merger into one great conifer forest? Or do we say ... 'Plant conifers for utility and profit if need be ... in places suitable for them, such as the more gloomy parts of the north of England and forbid their planting in the park landscape of the Midlands and the South.'

And the writer adds wistfully:

A strong argument could no doubt be made in favour of the older landscape, on grounds of attracting 'hard' tourist currency.

The schizophrenia which had troubled Repton was still active in the national psyche over a century later.

Moreover there was something about the moral earnestness of the whole Morris-Howard-Geddes-Mumford line of thought which was peculiarly unattractive to the more sophisticated European architects of the 1930s. Thus to Goodhart-Rendel functionalism was nothing better than

a close architectural analogue of puritanism, with its insistence on moral values, its distaste for aesthetic values, its righteous slow-wittedness and its abhorrence of gaiety.★

The fact that he had in mind German *modernismus*, and that the 'wit' so often paraded by neo-Georgian architects was nothing more than the last twitches of the corpse of the classical tradition, does not invalidate the criticism. Howard's image of the new city was so naïve, and Geddes's so insubstantial, that they had virtually no influence on the macro-aesthetics of urban design. They operated at the suburban scale. In the hands of Camillo Sitte in Germany, Unwin, Lutyens and Adshead in England, and Henry Wright and Clarence Stein in the USA, townplanning was a domestic art that made only minor demands on the imagination

★ H.S. Goodhart-Rendel, *Vitruvian Nights* (1932).

and no impact whatever on the apocalyptic situation in the great cities.

So we came out of the Second World War with a philosophy of conservation that had proved its utility in the United States and a philosophy of building that was to prove its utility in England. Founded by the great iconoclasts and hammered out in the simplistic atmosphere and long periods of boredom generated by the war, both had their deficiencies even in the narrow sectors in which they were tried. But their greatest deficiency was their inability to measure up to the built environment as a whole.

One can identify two main reasons. The first was the superficiality and lack of social relevance of the whole bundle of urban imagery that stretches from the Futurists to Le Corbusier. In the phrase of the 1940s, these people had not done their homework. Between the social intuitions of Howard and Geddes and the visual intuitions of Sant'Elia and Le Corbusier stretched a gulf which neither party had the capacity to bridge. The British failed to translate their concern for people into city design, and the continentals failed to think of their *Villes Radieuses* in terms of people. All this had been only too apparent when the British MARS group published its war-time plan for London. This should have bridged the gulf or at least recognised its existence, but it turned out to be a piece of vintage Futurism. The immense, obstinately defended urban region was to vanish under a sea of Corb-like parkscape, in which the faint forms of a few familiar monuments like St Paul's could just be discerned among the squiggles of vegetation. A brand-new armature of railways and motorways threading a score of brand-new linear cities would take its place. As for the parameters, needs and wants, site and scene, above all economics, they were beneath notice. Perhaps the technology was available, if you could isolate it, though even this seemed doubtful when the rain ran upwards through the mastic joints of the prototype UN building in New York.

The second reason for the failure to produce a viable theory of city design was that in the one country where planning *techniques* and powers were available, planning *ideas* and imagination on the scale required were not. The regulative and routine character of British planning goes right back into Victorian social history. In traditional British theory, government intervention in social problems (and they saw it as a social problem) must be limited to the role of umpire and first aid in dispute or distress; and in traditional British practice, urban problems came within the province of the Borough Engineer, who was the only official statutorily responsible for the physical state of the urban fabric. Overcrowding, slum clearance, zoning, densities, water supply and drainage, street works and public open spaces – all the raw material of planning was in his hands and in his head, and operated in his style and phraseology. Engineers by training tend to narrow their brief down to problems they can solve, whereas architects tend to widen it to issues beyond their sole capacity. Since the engineers were there, and the architects were not, urban problems had long since been narrowed down to a long, dull but manageable list. Nowadays the list is longer, the scope is greater, but British planning remains nine-tenths routine.

Yet the wartime generation of architect-planners had high hopes of a break-out. Encouraged first by Reith and later by Silkin to 'plan boldly', and inspired by the devoted and tireless Patrick Abercrombie, some of the blitzed cities commissioned highly coloured reconstruction plans, of which London's were the most comprehensive, Plymouth's the most grandiose, Coventry's the most realistic, and Thomas Sharp's picture-books of Durham, Oxford and Exeter the most sensitive. The analytic method used in these plans owed much to Geddes, and the solutions were Howard's and Unwin's. The strategy, in other words, was to break the urban mass down into village communities and decant the overspill to satellites; and the style was mini-Beaux Arts, with axial vistas, low buildings symmetrically grouped round traffic islands, avenues, shopping precincts (a word coined just before the war by the policeman Alker Tripp), tidily zoned industrial estates and generous green acreages. Nobody knew what it would cost or how it would be paid for, but the general and probably correct idea was to establish the aims first and let the methods follow from them.

So far so good. The trouble was that almost nothing derived from systematically established parameters. The community structures in the big cities were picked off the map and not from social surveys. The roads were guesswork unsupported by traffic projections or assignments. The shopping centres were often without servicing yards or parking for shoppers. The housing was Garden-City and quite alien in scale and texture to the dense urban scene in which it was to be set. The playing fields were the wishful thought of a charitable organisation. As for the economics, planners were pained and shocked if they were mentioned. But what mattered most about all this and finally sank these projects was not so much their immature science (which was perfectible) but their obsolete art, which turned its back on the entire machine-age aesthetic. These planners repudiated futurism, yet had wholly lost the wavelength of the past. Their pretty bird's eye views were literally meaningless.

The result was that when the 1947 Planning Act was introduced to enable it all to happen, it was none of it wanted, either by the man in the street or by the younger generation of architects. Planning became a decent dull job, nine-tenths administrative and defensive, and architects moved out of it *en masse* into the role which since the earliest days of modernism had always suited them best: the offensive. Undeterred, the planners proceeded to build up a formidable corpus of conventional wisdom. Like all such, this was a set of half-truths, the easier half being chosen.

The unstated but subsumed aim was to get back to the pre-industrial landscape of rural England, with towns of manageable size islanded in an ocean of 'countryside'. Here hardwood trees (but not softwoods) were to be protected, by law if necessary, quickset hedges encouraged, wirescape discouraged, semi-detached houses frowned-on, concrete banned, local building materials supported and even subsidised in deserving cases. That nearly the whole of this doctrine conflicted with the economics and technics of the farmers and foresters who actually made and maintained the landscape was a fact that nobody could bear to face. Upon this broad and bosky bosom of rural England we were to place New Towns like jewels – not, for heaven's sake, cities.

It is now generally agreed that the large city leads only to social evil. It monopolises the cultural life of the region, and often the nation. Apart from its inherent evils of creating high death and low birth rates, and of breeding maladjusted social types, such as gangsters and 'wide boys', it makes a full life impossible for the ordinary decent citizen.*

This statement betrays the powerful influence the Garden City movement still exerted even on paid-up members of the modern movement like Frederick Gibberd, whose book *Town Design* is the most comprehensive and sensitive textbook of the conventional wisdom of the 1950s.

By that decade, Corbusian aesthetics had been absorbed into the doctrine. His beautiful acropolis project for St Dié (later to be the source of Chandigarh and Brasilia) was much admired, and lip-service was paid to the MARS plan for London, because it had been made by respected people, even though everybody knew it was meaningless. It was the aim of every bombed city, of every populous London suburb and New Town, to achieve a baby St Dié, that is to say a central space marked by as tall a tower of civic offices as could be afforded, with town-hall, wedged-shaped concert hall or theatre, museum and art gallery. Gibberd specifically states that

The town centre is a composition in its own right, and for that composition to have a unity it will require a dominant element or crown.

This is Bruno Taut's *Stadtkrone*, faithfully copied by Unwin at Hampstead Garden Suburb, and of course it is a piece of pure romanticism, as impracticable in a modern city of office blocks and tower flats as it was unnecessary in historic examples of all scales from Paris (unless we are to regard the Eiffel Tower as a necessity) down to Cambridge and Cheltenham.

What happened in practice was that the municipalities could not

* Frederick Gibberd, *Town Design* (1953).

afford their *Stadtkrone*, and the gap was filled by the commercial developers with their shopping precincts and tower blocks. For these developers the conventional wisdom prescribed a 'plot ratio' (the multiple by which the floor space might exceed the site area) which combined with rigid daylighting standards to force developers on small sites to build high rather than wide. Ostensibly a parameter, these standards really enshrined an image – the image of the slim glass tower invented by Mies and featured in all Le Corbusier's studies in urbanism. It soon became apparent, particularly in London, that the convention which allowed plot ratios to exceed by ten per cent those which had existed on a site before the war, was producing hugely profitable buildings which were grossly out of scale with London and neither slim nor glassy. The incredible slowness with which the authorities reacted to this situation can perhaps only be decently accounted for by their subconscious obsession with the image of the glass tower. Certainly the office slab on its two-storey podium, of which Lever House in New York was the prototype, became the signature of the 1950s as universally as the semi-detached house had been that of the 20s.

It was its successful assault on the 'semi' which the conventional wisdom regarded as its first post-war achievement, but its own panacea, the two-storey terrace or row-house, was soon seen in the New Towns to threaten a new monotony. The solution put forward was 'mixed development', with a preponderance of low-rise housing 'punctuated' by the odd tower of flats for those who could be appropriately so housed. The watchword was 'urbanity', a word with Georgian connotations which embraced intimate enclosed spaces, hard paving rather than lawns, native trees rather than ornamental species and the suppression, within the limits of the possible, of the motor-car and the generous radii and sightlines it imposed. This last led to argument between architects and engineers which given the implacable growth of car ownership the former were bound, in the long run, to lose. On a broader front too it gradually became clear that 'urbanity' was not desired by those who had the economic power to choose: these, except in sophisticated metropolitan circles, invariably preferred suburbanity. Finally, mixed development was expensive because it was hard to standardise, low in density for urban sites, and dependent for its success on a high standard of layout and landscape. As urban land became scarcer and more costly the whole theory of providing the mixture that corresponded with human needs, let alone wants, broke down. Housing authorities fell back on the brutal expedient of package-deal skyscraper flats, and in doing so threw overboard the image of urbanity as well as most of the parameters.

One can sum up the rest of the conventional wisdom in the one word *segregation*. At all scales, this required the classification of land use by criteria which were seldom defined. There were National Parks, where wild scenery and recreational use were supposed to predominate; but farmers had to make a living in them and the nation was not rich enough (nor dictatorial enough in resisting local pressures) to ban from them extractive industries or nuclear power stations. There were Areas of Outstanding Natural Beauty and Areas of High Landscape Value, and later on in the towns there were Conservation Areas, where the aesthetic controls were supposed to operate with special force and concern for detail; but in practice they operated everywhere with an enthusiasm which some of the best (and some of the worst) architects found intolerable. There were industrial estates into which it was the policy to move 'non-conforming' industries out of housing areas. There were housing estates carefully segregated into public and private sectors, where pedestrians were supposed (though they did not want) to circulate on paths segregated from motor traffic in the manner developed in the eastern United States. And in town and city centres there were shopping precincts segregated horizontally from traffic and pedestrian deck systems segregated vertically, none of which were very popular. One of the great disappointments of the 1960s was the failure in public appeal of the 'Route 11' development in the City of London, where for the first time in England pure Corbusian principles were applied to an area of sufficient size by a group of talented planners brought up in the heart of the modern movement.

You can actually walk round the area today and see a planning dream carried out in much the same way as it had originally been visualised.

Percy Johnson-Marshall writes without irony, in a volume* which, like Gibberd's, comprehensively records the great projects of the 1950s and illustrates the social idealism which motivated his generation. For all that, it was undeniable that the imagery of the *Ville Radieuse* had begun to lose its force.

It is easy, but it would be unfair, to disparage the efforts of the men of the 1950s. This was the first generation to be adequately equipped, in terms of both ideas and technics, to get to grips with the urban jungle left by the Victorians. In its youth it had lived through the traumatic experience of the Great Depression, of fascism, and of world war, so that it possessed both moral imperatives and a proper sense of scale. Having grown up in the shadow of the pioneers Wright, Gropius, Mies and Le Corbusier, it had absorbed their message but reacted from their methods in the direction of group-working and anonymity. The modern movement – words which still had a meaning to them – was no longer a battle-cry but the air they breathed.

It seems likely that the most useful achievements of the 1950s, none of which really matured until the 1960s, were three. First, they transformed the scale of the notion of New Towns, which was still Edwardian in tone when they inherited it. By the time they had finished with it, it had mutated into new city-regions involving a redeployment of population and employment on a national scale. The flow of new life into Clydeside, Tyne-Tees and Merseyside, where some of the best new communities and urban renewal projects were initiated, was the first serious attempt to reverse the inter-war drift to the south-east. Second, they went to work on the slums and evolved, particularly in London, patterns of new housing and community services which for all their deficiencies were more human than those to be found in any other comparable city. The size of the renewal problem, which at the beginning of the period seemed almost as immeasurable as India's, was seen by

* Percy Johnson-Marshall, *Rebuilding Cities* (1966).

its end to be manageable: it was a good sign that by then it was less its operational than its philosophical aspects that were causing concern. Third, this generation was the first to apply scientific method to traffic analysis and management, so that the work of Buchanan and others was able to command almost instantaneous and universal acceptance. The generation which had begun by ending the reign of the semi-detached house went on to end the reign of the multi-purpose street. The concept of a transportation hierarchy, and of roads as totally and inconspicuously integrated with buildings as pipes and wires, was now available as a theory, even though nobody could see how the scale of the operation could be manageable in practice.

Steady progress seemed discernible – as steady as the world of the Enlightenment when it was assaulted by the Romantic Movement, as steady as the *Belle Epoque* when it was destroyed by war. The catalyst this time was the young New York journalist Jane Jacobs, whose book *The Death and Life of Great American Cities** was coolly and craftily calculated to demolish item by item the fabric of the conventional wisdom. 'A city can not be a work of art': in this flat statement alone Mrs Jacobs denies the pretensions of all those pattern-makers and prima donna planners from Scamozzi to Lucio Costa.

> To approach a city, or even a city neighbourhood, as if it were a larger architectural problem, capable of being given order by converting it into a disciplined work of art, is to make the mistake of attempting to substitute art for life.

She goes on to describe the infinite complexity and diversity of a city's activities in the familiar language of the Usonian critique of formalism, derived from Rousseau and put into architectural terms by Frank Lloyd Wright: 'why do you not trust life?' 'Radiant Garden City Beautiful' is the devastating phrase in which she lumps together the good intentions of all the chairborne paper planners of the last two generations. To her the City of Tomorrow is wholly unwanted. In a characteristic passage she extols the slums.

* Jane Jacobs, *The Death and Life of Great American Cities* (1961).

In the Back-of-the-Yards, Chicago, no weather-beaten, undistinguished, run-down, presumably obsolete frame house seems to be too far gone to lure out savings and to instigate borrowing – because this is a neighbourhood that people are not leaving as they achieve enough success for choice . . .

At the other extreme, in Miami Beach, where novelty is the sovereign remedy, hotels ten years old are considered aged and are passed up because others are newer. Newness, and its superficial gloss of well-being, is a very perishable commodity.

Many city occupants and enterprises have no need for new construction. The floor of the building in which this book is being written is occupied also by a health club with a gym, a firm of ecclesiastical decorators, an insurgent Democratic party reform club, a Liberal party political club, a music society, an accordionists' association, a retired importer who sells maté by mail, a man who sells paper and who also takes care of shipping the maté, a dental laboratory, a studio for watercolor lessons, and a maker of costume jewelry. Among the tenants who were here and gone shortly before I came in, were a man who rented out tuxedos, a union local and a Haitian dance troupe. There is no place for the likes of us in new construction.*

So much for urban renewal. There were other heresies:

> Children like playing on footways and not in playgrounds.
> Open space has no intrinsic value.
> Parks are areas of danger: they should be central and not peripheral.
> Civic centres are dead concepts: social buildings should be dispersed.
> City housing projects create brutal environments.
> Comprehensive rebuilding is a mistake: investment should be an irrigation, not a flood.
> Urban motorways do not promote renewal: they promote decay.

This was, of course, the other half of the truth, the difficult half. It left planners of all shapes and sizes stunned or angry, because it offered no solutions, or none that they believed would work. It was a job of pure demolition, expertly carried out by an amateur. The conventional wisdom has never recovered.

It was not long before Jane Jacobs' intuitions were taken up and rationalised into a theory of urban structure on which it might be

* Jacobs, *Great American Cities*.

possible to build. This was done by a young British mathematician and architect working in America, Christopher Alexander. In a brilliant essay published in 1964 he noted the perplexing failure of artificial cities and new towns to create an environment in which people could feel happy and fulfilled, and asked himself what Welwyn and Stevenage and Greenbelt and Chandigarh and Brasilia could possibly have in common. He found that they were all based on a hierarchical deployment of all their components – roads, neighbourhoods, schools, social buildings, open spaces. 'Big fleas have little fleas on their backs to bite 'em. Little fleas have smaller fleas and so ad infinitum.' He called this structure a tree. In old cities, on the other hand, life was not organised in this way: people would shop in one district, take their children to school in another, go out to dinner in a third, creating a criss-cross of movement and a complex overlap of areas of use. He called this structure a semi-lattice. It was of course a much more sophisticated structure.

This enormously greater variety is an index of the great structural complexity a semi-lattice can have when compared with the structural simplicity of a tree. It is this lack of structural complexity, characteristic of trees, which is crippling our conceptions of the city.*

Here are two characteristic applications of the theory. The first is about friendship:

Whenever we have a tree structure it means that within this structure no piece of any unit is ever connected to other units, except through the medium of that unit as a whole.

The enormity of this restriction is difficult to grasp. It is a little as though the members of a family were not free to make friends outside the family, except when the family as a whole made a friendship.

But today's social structure is utterly different. If we ask a man to name his friends and then ask them in turn to name their friends, they will all name different people, very likely unknown to the first person; these people would again name others, and so on outwards. There are virtually no closed groups of people in modern society. The reality of

* Christopher Alexander, 'A City is not a Tree', *Architectural Forum* (April and May 1964).

85

today's social structure is thick with overlap – the systems of friends and acquaintances form a semi-lattice, not a tree.

The second is about traffic:

Imagine yourself coming out of a Fifth Avenue store: you have been shopping all afternoon; your arms are full of parcels; you need a drink; your wife is limping. Thank God for taxis!

Yet the urban taxi can function only because pedestrians and vehicles are not strictly separated. The prowling taxi needs a fast stream of traffic so that it can cover a large area to be sure of finding a passenger. The pedestrian needs to be able to hail the taxi from any point in the pedestrian world, and to be able to get out to any part of the pedestrian world to which he wants to go. The system which contains the taxicabs needs to overlap both the fast vehicular traffic system and the system of pedestrian circulation.

In a final image of the dissociation wrought by the planner's ideal of segregation, he takes the problem of old age:

An ominous example of city-wide dissociation is the separation of retired people from the rest of urban life, caused by the growth of desert cities for the old, like Sun City, Arizona. This separation is only possible under the influence of tree-like thought.

It not only takes from the young the company of those who have lived long, but worse, it causes the same rift inside each individual life. As you yourself pass into Sun City, and into old age, your ties with your own past will be unacknowledged, lost, and therefore broken. Your youth will no longer be alive in your old age – the two will be dissociated, your own life will be cut in two.

For the human mind, the tree is the easiest vehicle for complex thoughts. But the city is not, cannot, and must not be a tree. The city is a receptacle for life. If the receptacle severs the overlap of the strands of life within it, because it is a tree, it will be like a bowl full of razor blades on edge, ready to cut up whatever is entrusted to it. In such a receptacle life will be cut to pieces. If we make cities which are trees, they will cut your life within to pieces.

Meanwhile the reaction against the whole ideology and effort of the 1950s was gathering pace. This was not of course a mass movement: mass opinion, as far as could be judged, was cynical or conformist. It was an uneasy alliance of middle-class extremes, of old-guard preservationists on the right who had never liked the modern movement anyway, and of the whiz-kids of pop culture on the left. Thus the London geographer, Peter Hall, could write in pure nostalgia of the slum-clearance campaign in the black cities of the English north:

These motorways, sometimes elevated, sometimes depressed in trenches, are being constructed through the most amazing scenes of devastation ever witnessed by the people of England. The Luftwaffe never achieved anything like it. The nearest parallel is Dresden, or even Hiroshima, in 1945. In the great cities of the north, whole areas have been razed to the ground, almost as far as the eye can see. At most, a few pubs survive as a sentimental concession to the past; often, the people displaced from the houses round about to far flung peripheral estates come back on Saturday nights to them.

Though not all cities are the same, in many of them the new land-scape that is put on this blank map is the same. Huge industrialised blocks, up to 20, 30 even 40 storeys high, tower into the skies.*

But the remedy was not to be sought, as Alexander had proposed, in deeper understanding of the good qualities of these old cities embodied in more sophisticated planning techniques. Planning as such was now the public enemy.

The monuments of our century that have spontaneity and vitality are found not in the old cities, but in the American west.

There, in the desert and the Pacific states, creations like Fremont Street in Las Vegas or Sunset Strip in Beverly Hills represent the living architecture of our age.†

The pop-art of the 'swinging sixties' lay to hand as the best possible stick with which to beat up the 'good taste' of the older generation. Its West-Coast-American imagery of gas stations, motels, wild advertising, flashing neon and ribbon-development was precisely what all the best people had for half a century been defending rural England against.

A lot of this was good fun, not taken too tragically by its

* Peter Hall, 'Monumental Folly', *New Society*, 24 October 1968.
† Peter Hall, 'Spontaneity and Space', *New Society*, 20 March 1969.

victims. But the collapse of confidence was real enough, and few would dispute Alexander's sad conclusion:

Architects themselves admit more and more freely that they really like living in old buildings more than new ones. The non-art-loving public at large, instead of being grateful to architects for what they do, regards the onset of modern buildings and modern cities everywhere as an inevitable, rather sad piece of the larger fact that the world is going to the dogs.*

Macro-aesthetics – the attempt to make sense of the whole human environment – seemed to have ceased to exist.

* Alexander, 'A City is not a Tree'.

5

The Waste Land

It was a journey of six-and-thirty hours. I had set out from Whitcross on a Tuesday afternoon, and early on the succeeding Thursday morning the coach stopped to water the horses at a wayside inn, situated in the midst of scenery whose green hedges and large fields and low pastoral hills (how mild of feature and verdant of hue compared with the stern North-Midland moors of Morton!) met my eye like the lineaments of a once familiar face. Yes, I knew the character of this landscape: I was sure we were near my bourne.

'How far is Thornfield Hall from here?' I asked of the ostler.

'Just two miles, ma'am, across the fields.'

'My journey is closed,' I thought to myself. I got out of the coach, gave a box I had into the ostler's charge, to be kept until I called for it; paid my fare; satisfied the coachman, and was going: the brightening day gleamed on the sign of the inn, and I read in gilt letters, 'The Rochester Arms'. My heart leapt up: I was already on my master's very lands.★

For many years the bane of passenger handling – at least from the passengers' viewpoint – has been the fact that loading an airplane cannot be accomplished with protection from the elements. Extensible canvas awnings were used at a few airports with meager success. The ubiquitous umbrella almost lent a touch of comedy to the loading process as passenger and agent leaped among the puddles in a dash toward the cabin door.

Recently a device has been developed with the intent of alleviating the loading problem; it is similar to the locomotive transfer table in

★ Charlotte Brontë, *Jane Eyre*.

general use in railroad repair shops. It consists of a pair of tracks each of which supports a dolly. The airplane taxis onto a dolly with each of its main tires, and is then brought toward the loading gate by means of electric-powered cables. Projecting from the terminal is a fixed two-storey 'finger' with, at its outer end, a short ramp which can be adjusted to varying cabin sill heights.

In addition to permitting the loading of passengers or cargo to proceed on a level and under cover, use of this device permits a number of changes which should increase the efficiency of terminal operation.*

Things like this meanwhile had been going wrong in the world, changes beyond the traditional sphere of architecture in which nevertheless architects had played an enthusiastic part. All journeys had become too easy. The minutely farmed countrysides of Western Europe, formerly netted by an intimate system of field-paths worn smooth by women returning from shopping, men from work, children from school, were now redundant and choked with brambles in all the corners into which machinery could not penetrate. The bright spots of human dawdlers or pick-nickers that Monet loved had vanished from the hayfields. Along the lane in which the Rev Francis Kilvert rode to call on a sick parishioner, noting on the way a child's expression, a new flower in the hedgerow, the larks in the sky, the panel doctor now drove in his superbly sealed Rover 2000 with the Archers on the car radio. Huge tin signs told him the name of the next village. And the sick man did not die: it was harder than ever before to die.

Hurtling across the sky in pressurized containers, elderly American ladies could reach the ruins of Angkor, deep in the impenetrable Cambodian jungle, from any of the world's conurbations in under twenty-four hours. In the time it takes to drink a quarter bottle of champagne and eat a plastic meal, the Northerner could be switched from a fogbound polder to an olive grove ringing with cicadas. That long drive from Calais endlessly southwards, the sun strengthening every day, from cornfields into vineyards into limestone ravines into red earth and olives, until finally one sunset the first lighthouses of the Mediterranean could be seen

* *Architectural Review* (January 1951).

flashing in the misty distance; the progression backwards into history from Gothic through Romanesque to the Roman ruins themselves; the eternal symbolic journey from the periphery to the centre, which Samuel Johnson called the 'prime object of travelling' – all this had become so easy to skip that it seemed an affectation to give time to it. The first lizard, the first firefly, the first cork-oak – now we get them in one package like frozen vegetables, those tasteless travesties that mark our triumph over time as well as space.

Palaeotechnic industrialism did not at first seem to be headed in this direction. The great transcontinental expresses, moaning through the Middle-Western night or panting at tiny French stations in the small hours, while small horns blew and water was taken on, or clanging in immensely tall above the sleeping multitudes on Indian platforms – these 'monsters' were spoken of as swallowing up the miles, but in fact through their intensification of movement they created space. For vast numbers the metropolitan termini truly were what they called themselves – the gateways to the world. Not for nothing are St Petersburg and Vienna carved on the entrance piers of Blackfriars Station. The long hard night through the heart of Europe, the grind over the Alps, the Italian customs, the soft drinks from Bohemian villages, the change of menu and personnel in the dining-car, the peeling off one by one of the bronze-lettered carriages of the *Compagnie Internationale des Wagons Lits et des Grands Express Européens* as the train wound on towards Constantinople – this was to the middle-class Victorians a far richer experience than the milords in their carriages could ever have had.

For those who lived as we did on an island, every journey began with the splendours and miseries of the sea. It would be absurd to sentimentalise the Channel crossing or the transatlantic liner with its vulgar contrast between the permed ladies in the bars and the emigrants in the hold. Ships always had been brutal communities in which their isolation in the elemental wastes had seemed to magnify all the distresses of mankind. But what an arrival, or departure! At all scales, from the complex tie-up at the feet of the skyscrapers and a stone's throw from the sedans on their endless conveyor belt on Riverside Drive, to the chartered ketch chugging into a Mediterranean or Caribbean port at dawn, with only the bakers at work in the shadowed streets: not lost to us, all this, but now a rich man's pleasure, like a bottle of wine to an Englishman. Even more moving were the departures, with a small band playing at the pier end and the gap of water between the dockside and the great wall of the ship ineluctably widening; and then in the Atlantic swell 'the last of England' dissolving into the stormy dusk. In exchange our technology has given us the impeccable automation of the airport, with passengers absorbed like a raw material, processed, packaged, and consigned to an identical outlet in any continent. Only at the remotest airstrips does the festive arrival of the weekly plane convey some hint of what travel used to be like.

Edward Lear's journals convey as well as any both the distresses of the voyage and their enhancement of vision. Even on the short night crossing to Corsica:

He is fortunate, who after ten hours of sea passage can reckon up no worse memories than those of a passive condition of suffering – of that dislocation of mind and body ... when the outer man is twisted and rolled and jerked, and the movements of thought seem more or less to correspond with those of the body. Wearily go by 'the slow sad hours that bring us all things ill'.★

But then an arrival:

Extreme beauty of Bombay harbour. At 7 leave the *India* in a steam tug. No trouble anywhere. Violent and amazing delight at the wonderful variety of life and dress hue. Exquisite novelties, flowers, trees ... O new palms! O flowers! O creatures! O beasts! Anything more overpoweringly amazing cannot be conceived. Colours and costumes and myriadism of impossible picturesqueness!†

Lear drew the world as he wanted it to be: the peaks a little more elegant than the reality, the clumps of trees more richly

★ Edward Lear, *Journal of a Landscape Painter in Corsica* (1868).
† Edward Lear, *Indian Journal* (1873).

Georgian, the peasants more picturesquely grouped – the same licence by which twentieth-century artists make it more menacing, more absurd, or more honky-tonk. We know that in the 1860s half-timbered hydros like monstrous Mayerlings had started to occupy every viewpoint, railways to cut every romantic valley to ribbons, civic vulgarity to tear the guts out of every decent market-place. And in a corner of the mind must always have been the dark world of Doré's London slums. 'The poor are always with us.' Lear's was merely the appropriate half of the truth, appropriate because he was celebrating, like so many Victorian artists, the end of the unified eotechnic world. His lonely uncomfortable cab-rides pursued the same quarry as the package tours of today.

This is a search that cannot succeed. Every summer that sees a new egg-crate hotel open in a new cove it becomes harder. Every airstrip on a new island has that particular eotechnic survival corrupted in a predictable number of years. The new flight that tempts the rich man to build his summer place brings the coach tour and the amplified pop group that forces him to shut his windows on windless nights. The only peasants left with a shred of national costume and a donkey are octogenarians. For a time an orderly withdrawal inland seems to meet the case, with a blue pool substituting for the sea and a few jokes about the empty *Ambre Solaire* containers on the sea floor, horribly magnified by the snorkel goggles. But when this becomes a ten-mile climb on to an arid and treeless mountainside most of the *douceur de vivre* has fallen away. We are approaching the point of time when the only quiet places are unfit for habitation and the only solitary journeys are in the most unpleasant places on earth.

Thus, perhaps unregretted, dies the privileged nostalgic tourist's-eye view of the world. For to everybody else the utopia of the television commercials is positively and actively desired. The Chinese shopkeeper in his dark cavern wants that blue-white fluorescent strip; the Cretan bar-owner wants his deep-freeze to contain the fruit-flavoured yoghurt; the African schoolgirl passionately desires the mini-skirt and rejects those graceful ankle-length wrap-around prints. Noise as such, for so long the special taste of the urban Italians, is now cultivated by the formerly silent Turks, Japs and Amerindians. The smallest tribal territory must now have its airline and a six-lane highway to the airport with oleanders in the central strip. The flower before the plant, the two-tone bathroom before the water-supply.

In the British Isles, whose landscapes still celebrated a better-balanced view of the world, this was a particularly regressive development. The countryside left to us by the Age of Reason had been created on two principles. The first was that utility and beauty went hand in hand. The High Farming introduced by Coke of Norfolk was the physical and economic base for the great house at Holkham and the immense vistas planned by Kent and Capability Brown. All over the country those flat-faced squires with their long-barrelled shot-guns were eager to do what Pope and Walpole told them: aesthetes and philistines had not yet been invented. The second principle was the submission of the present to the future. It is easy to forget, when we read literary evocations of the Arcadian scene, that they never saw it: it existed in their imaginations; what they saw were stringy saplings in fenced clumps and broad stretches of gorsy heathland, that 'open country' (in the words of Walpole's famous encomium on William Kent) 'on which a landscape might be designed'. Perhaps it is this knowledge which makes the best of our park-like landscapes so poignant, when on windless evenings of high summer those monumental elms rise out of the white fields like accusers and the sheep against the light recall Samuel Palmer and Thomas Hardy and the lost eotechnic unities. We are the hollow men.

Out to the west of most European capitals are the *pavillons*, the *Lustschlösser*, the *dachas* and the villas of the old aristocracies, and these have now become a nice drive on a summer evening, if you can stand the traffic blocks on the way. None is more attractive or more accessible than Chiswick House, Lord Burlington's much loved and exquisite miniature combining the styles of Palladio and Scamozzi, described unkindly by Lord Hervey as 'too little to

live in, but too large to hang to one's watch'. Its classical/pictur-
esque garden, the masterpiece (with Rousham in Oxfordshire) of
William Kent, has grown familiar from the fashion photographs,
with models posed against a temple, an obelisk, or a sphinx.

The villa lies in the crook of a roaring highway interchange, and
you will take your life in your hands as you run across the road
to its main gate. At a glance one can see that the house and its
original east wing, with Wyatt's accretions swept away, have been
meticulously restored by the Ministry of Public Building and
Works. But the cedar avenue has not lasted well and gaps are
filled by saplings, some of which must have been destroyed by
vandals. The house stands on an apron of tarmac, patched where
drains, etc. have been lately repaired. Off to the left, Kent's wavy
canal, now dirty and weedy, can be seen through a newly-
repaired chain-link fence. Beyond where the water used to merge
with the dark groves, there is another line of chain-link fencing,
squashed in places where determined couples have got through.
Litter baskets stand in conspicuous places on the tired grass and so
does loose litter. What is left of the Portland stone balustrade of
the beautiful humped bridge has had to be railed off with more
much-savaged chain-link, so that the rest of it shall not be pushed
into the water. Every few seconds the melancholy scene is flooded
by the deafening noise of jet airliners on the last stages of their
approach run to Heathrow.

There are times when our forebodings become unbearable and
we share D. H. Lawrence's sense of doom when he wrote on the
eve of war:

> When I drive across this country with autumn falling and rustling to
> pieces, I am so sad, for my country, for this great wave of civilisation,
> two thousand years, which is now collapsing, that it is hard to live.

It was right and proper that the British were the first to develop
and perfect a planning methodology that could stop the rot. The
means were to hand, but it was the ends which had gone sour.
Alternative scenarios were available, but none of them made
complete and convincing sense. So policy lurched from side to

side roughly on a generation time scale. One generation set up Green Belts; the next filled them in. One generation passed a Restriction of Ribbon Development Act, the next declared for linear housing along minor roads. One generation created National Parks as areas of wild scenery and solitude; the next moved large-scale industry into them.

The result was a general entropy and dilution of local identity. Whatever the local tradition of living and building, multi-storey housing suppressed it because it was technically the simplest way of achieving quantity without getting mixed up in the complex infrastructure problems of new communities. Countries exchanged tower block technology in the same way as they exchanged motor-cars. So the British, ancestral gardeners endowed with the perfect gardening climate, cooped themselves up in sky-flats which Mediterranean peoples only endured because they were traditionally underprivileged and Scandinavians only accepted because they had the resources in land and money for weekend and summer cottages.

These structures were as disappointing aesthetically as socially. Their 'endless architecture' presented blank expressionless faces in all directions, since neither Corbusian modelling nor Miesian transparency met their needs. They were not tall enough to mix with the atmosphere or dominate the city form in the manner of the Ville Radieuse. The most they could manage was a local 'accent', and this was weakened by their enforced similarity and frequent repetition: there was nothing local about them. On the other hand they were too tall and faceless to be ingredients in the rich and exciting confections projected by Sant'Elia and still powerful in pop-art imagery. They offered nothing to exploration, no possibility of a surprise. True, they cleared some ground, tearing up some of the grey or red carpet of Victorian housing that had made the larger English cities the drabbest places on earth. But the ground they cleared was too intensively cultivated for car-parking, play areas, laundries and other utilities to permit of that free and bold modelling and planting that was the secret of the manmade English landscape and the desperate deficiency of the English industrial town. By and large they created across the world an urban desert of concrete or tarmac or parched earth, regimented or lawless according to local custom and standards of living. Because it was Everyman's land, it was a no-man's land, flouting the Territorial Imperative.

But the old grade-level English suburbia that looks so good from the air, doesn't work either. It too has to be done well to be worth doing, and this we cannot afford. Small communities – no larger than Hampstead Garden Suburb – with space for large trees, twice as many cars as houses, sports clubs and meeting places, swimming pools and one-level supermarkets and a range of schools, all within a decent ride of employment, are for the prosperous only in even the richest countries. This kind of property is theft, in Proudhon's phrase, because it diverts resources from areas where need is infinitely greater and from people who cannot buy these things for themselves. Such suburbs, linked to downtown by an elevated expressway striding across the roofs of the Negro inner ring, are one of the central paradigms of social injustice.

And this central area, when you reach it? Nowadays it is a noise sewer. Of course towns have always been noisy, and smelly. Without these human characteristics they would be sinister, like a Chirico. The trouble is that the noise has become wholly inorganic and inhuman, as well as ten times greater in mere decibels. Sports cars and motorcycles make it worse on purpose. Buchanan defined an excessive noise level as one in which it was impossible for two people to have an intelligent conversation, or gossip come to that, in the street: this now applies to all the popular and crowded streets in the world's cities except Venice. At home, aeroplanes make it equally impossible in a summer garden.

A second new feature, connected of course with the first, is the depopulation of the centre. In this movement the British industrial towns led the way. Workshops had to be within walking distance of workers and in due course this produced an environment from which anyone who could afford any kind of transport must escape. First the railway and then the motor-car speeded up the centrifuge, and more workshops, shops and offices filled the gaps. The final pattern in all the western world's major provincial cities was a downtown area consisting solely of commercial buildings and parking lots, silent as the desert at night, an inner ring or grey area of the underprivileged who could afford nothing better, and a commuting belt extending up to 100 miles in which ninety per cent of the working population lived at subtly different shades of density and sophistication. The most prosperous lived outside the city boundaries and contributed nothing to its revenues or its leadership.

In the American cities where this pattern was best exemplified, spasmodic efforts to reverse the trend had been made. The commercial core was generally too expensive to touch, and was left to reflect the market economy as it had always vividly and brutally done. Public money was concentrated on an attempt to clean up the worst sections of the grey area and to attract back into it some of the people who had fled the city and could afford an economic rent for the new flats and row houses. Urban renewal thus earned for itself the synonym 'Negro removal' and produced social stresses worse than those it set out to alleviate. The resulting backlash is passionately described by Jane Jacobs.

London, Paris and New York in varying degrees escaped this fate for several reasons. They were none of them primarily industrial cities and while never obstructing industrial development were able to hold it at arm's length, out of sight, downwind. As centres of government or world trade or culture or all three, they attracted the ambitious and were the working habitat of the rich, many of whom found it convenient to live near their work and could afford to. And they extended so far that the alternative of commuting through a huge suburban belt to a better environment was less attractive. Even so, as the running cost of their immense infrastructures descended more and more heavily on the ratepayers in their central areas, the same centrifugal movement of the population was apparent in them all and could at any moment get out of control.

On the whole, perhaps because it had the longest experience of the problems of size, London coped best with these stresses. The rich stuck it out in the central area and so did the comparatively poor in their privileged council flats. The young of all nationalities found cracks in the urban fabric for their pads, picking up cheap fag ends of leases and moving on when the developers moved in. Professional families reconditioned the grey areas, sent their children to the comprehensive schools, and fought to the death against the Motorway Box: these were people who had learned the hard lesson that life is possible without a motor-car. With everybody's goodwill, the authorities clamped down on central area parking and made the historic core of London the only western metropolitan centre in which one could walk or ride without too much discomfort or frustration.

Most of what was squalid and vulgar about Victorian London had been swept away with the famous fogs and the city now shone brightly under the vast skies of summer evenings, across which a steady stream of airliners whined down to Heathrow. But the rebuilt areas disappointed everybody. The mere bulk of modern buildings made them humanly oppressive and potentially destructive of such few good skylines as the city possessed: with only two of them alongside Hyde Park a philistine Minister, overruling all advice, was able to do more visual damage than two buildings had ever done before. And whereas on the whole the new commercial buildings were neither better nor worse as urban scenery than their predecessors, which had always been mainly dull, occasionally ugly and hardly ever distinguished, something had gone seriously wrong at their public level, in the areas with which people came in intimate contact. The new public spaces contributed at such vast expense and adorned with floorscape, water features and sculpture by the best names seemed no substitute for the wholly artless and often scruffy little streets and alleys of old London. Something hitherto unrecognised about the texture, complexity and spontaneity of unwilled townscape that had nothing to do with antiquity or 'architectural' value or picturesqueness in the long-admired Italian manner, suddenly seemed important, vulnerable and in need of care and protection. The developers, already on the defensive ever since they made their fortunes in the 1950s, found themselves harried harder than ever.

Behind the scenes, behind these square and pretentious concrete achievements, the strategic, structural problems of London were as menacing as ever. Despite the New Towns and controlled dispersal all over England south of the Trent, the conurbation still lacked the space to house its working population, let alone to provide the long-promised new parks and playing-fields. Like all the world's great employment magnets, the London region attracted people faster than it could house them, and being too tidy-minded to let them run up their own shacks on the outskirts, it could only offer an institutional bed and board in the grimmest Dickensian style, breaking up families and piling up ill-will. And as the city's working population expanded the load on its transport system, still the best and most humane in the world, increased. Projecting the car ownership trend, planners predicted the need for a £2,000 million motorway system by the 1990s which the urban fabric could only absorb at the cost of some of its newly-reconditioned and desperately needed houses, not to mention other unpleasant side-effects. A less conspicuous but equally ominous implication was that if we spent money of this order on motorways we could not spend it on public transport, yet unless we did its competitive efficiency must decline still further and reinforce the demand for more and more motorways. London could be headed straight for the vicious American spiral.

On the other hand the cost of monorails and other rapid-transit systems in the Futurist image was even more astronomical for an economy perpetually in a state of groggy medication. The huge and political question loomed up of whether to breach the dams and let the jobs and houses spread themselves, as in a market economy they undoubtedly would, all over the still beautiful and passionately protected countryside of southern England.

For despite all inroads it was still beautiful. At an ecological cost only perceptible to the initiated, agriculture continued to increase its productivity, the fields brimmed over with stiff and heavy-headed varieties of cereal, and the herds looked the best-fed in the world. As farms amalgamated, farmers tended to become middle-class businessmen; yet somehow, against all reason, even in the arable counties, the great hedgerow elms seemed to survive the bulldozers of December and the straw fires of September, and particularly in the green west the park-like English scene lingered on, over-ripe and all the finer for it. Powerful forces both bureaucratic and busybody went into action against bad husbandry or woodland management, and vernacular buildings however inefficient had somehow to be propped up and kept in use. As agricultural employment declined, the villages became increasingly (and uniquely in Europe) white-collar communities, and any cottage within an hour's drive of a job could be sure of repair and conversion of varying degrees of aptness or ineptitude. 'Best-kept village' competitions all over Britain ensured the nation-wide dissemination of suburban ideals.

Yet the forces arrayed against all these good intentions were formidable. Each new inter-city motorway that penetrated the local defences produced intense pressures in the area of each interchange, and if soil quality was below average and other factors favourable these could escalate into a new housing estate, an airport, or even a city. Power stations, power lines, the natural gas grid, reservoirs, sewage works, and all the rest of the apparatus of a technologically mature society added their quota. Even the greenbelts, the pride of an earlier generation of planners, had become so moth-eaten that there was a tendency to write them off as sacred cows in which mainstream planners and *avant-garde* architects for once saw eye to eye: it had become a left-wing fashion to refer to them as a protective device of the city golfing fraternity. Moreover it had become accepted policy in all the world's conurbations that the most functional and economical structure for future growth was the urban corridor or finger threaded by motorways and other rapid transit systems; this made nonsense of greenbelts based on a hiving-off principle which experience had shown to have severe economic limitations: there could never be enough mobile jobs to support many more remote satellites. And on top of the problem of growth was the physical fact that nearly half the population still lived at densities of over a hundred to the acre when the rest lived at six or less. In a society which would before long be 100 per cent motorized, could one treat this for ever, this age-old contrast between 'urban' and 'rural' man, as one of the immutable facts of life?

The trouble was that the country had long been notoriously unbalanced in the ratio of population to basic resources. Whereas the world as a whole, forgetting all forebodings, still had four acres of cultivable and habitable land per head in 1970 (as against an estimated minimum requirement of two and a half for cultivable land alone), Britain had less than an acre, with the urbanised element encroaching on the cultivable at the rate of 40,000 acres a year. In a world whose forests would at the present rate be wholly exhausted within a century, whereas the USA had four acres of forest per head, Britain had a twelfth of an acre. In so far as any such figures make sense in the midst of the population explosion, ours only made sense on the assumption of permanent surpluses in the rest of the world and our own continued ability to pay for them. Neither of these assumptions was safe, so that lip service was paid on all sides to the necessity for waste avoidance and multiple use. But we had grown rich on precisely the opposite principle, and prodigality had become a habit. All users claimed that waste avoidance and multiple use made unacceptable inroads on their competitive margins, and appealed as usual to a government which was too hard-up to be far-sighted. Still harder was it to find government money for the restoration to productive and recreational use of the country's 100,000 acres of existing industrial wasteland, even though all the paper plans and techniques were ready.

Superimposed on all these functional problems was the rapidly-expanding leisure industry, with a potential for doing small things in the wrong way which could be cumulatively disastrous as well as self-destructive. To the British, cooped up in their island, with their beauty spots already the worse for wear and the prospect of a car population tripled by the end of the century, this had become an obsession, perhaps excessively so, since jumbo tourist flights and a Channel Tunnel could well transfer the load elsewhere before long.

These prospects that worried the professionals lay mainly in the future, whereas the things that depressed the amateurs were only too tangibly present. Europe seemed overnight to have moved from an age of improvement into an age of deterioration. Since the Victorian proliferation of architects, country builders had lost the art of building and developed the habit of playing the idiot boy, just taking orders. So even the elementary small house built in traditional materials was now beyond their design capability, and an architect had to be brought in – and no ordinary architect: only a handful of exceptionally sensitive persons could be trusted with this simplest of all problems. These few were too busy to take it on.

To cope with this situation, Britain had set up an elaborate system of aesthetic controls, in which all sorts of amateurs could overrule such minimal professional advice as was available and try their hands at design correction. This eliminated some of the worst blunders and was probably worth having on that account, but it was powerless to raise the general level of ineptitude. In other countries, in particular in those Mediterranean ones which nature and history had always smiled on, even this palliative was lacking. Virtually no planning framework existed to take the shock of the development boom. Misgoverned Spain and Greece, even experienced Italy, merrily set about destroying the very qualities that attracted foreigners and supported their economies. By and large, such building controls as existed were traditionally in the hands of officially-employed engineers. In the days when technology was elementary and these elementary skills were universal this was a sinecure. Now that new development involved scrub-clearance, earth-moving, road-building, water collection or distribution, waste-disposal, overhead power lines and perhaps oil storage, gas mains and television, the job had become one of major landscape transformation, and virtually no local authorities employed anybody who could handle it.

So the bulldozers got loose in the Arcadian landscape and the jazz-modern villa, that international symbol of rising expectations, made its appearance in every cove that could raise a water supply, and around the fringes of every picturesque old town. The Indian, the African and the European versions were identical. Inside it were the equally international consumer durables and packaged foods that had banished so much of the drudgery and so much of the savour of life. Broiler-house chicken, frozen peas and fish fingers reflected the escalating priority of quantity over quality. Whereas factory farming, to many people's dismay, developed rapidly, the sea was still hunted palaeolithically at increasing distances and difficulties. In many small Mediterranean ports there were few fishermen left with a complete set of fingers, now that the grossly wasteful method of dynamiting was the last hope of getting a living out of the sea. Here was one among innumerable examples of that loss of physical contact between adversaries and allies which, originating in warfare and infinitely magnifying its inhumanity, now infected the primeval relationships between hunter and hunted, between man and his domestic animals, and between man and his neighbours in the natural world. Bewick in his *History of British Birds* (1797) writes of the Redbreast:

Its well-known familiarity has attracted the attention and secured the protection of men in all ages; it haunts the dwellings of the cottager and partakes of his humble fare; when the cold grows severe, and snow covers the ground, it approaches the house, taps at the window with its bill, as if to entreat an asylum, which is always cheerfully granted, and, with a simplicity the most delightful, hops round the house, picks up crumbs, and seems to make himself one of the family.

What robin now would ask to be admitted to the farmhouse kitchen with its whirring machinery and the day-long yackety-yack of Radio 2 on the transistor? Fortunately for their peace of mind it is hard for human beings to be aware of losses such as these. Over the world as a whole, those who were not dependent on subsistence agriculture for a wretched and precarious living were by now fully persuaded that a can of baked beans made better eating.

For with every year that passed governments and giant corporations were improving their techniques of persuasion. The mirror image of the arrogance of those who claim to meet society's unspoken needs is the arrogance of those who manipulate for their own benefit society's wants. As technology continually widened the gap between producer and consumer (originally one person, then for centuries one community) it became rarer and rarer to satisfy a need by one's own ingenuity. One's role became one of choice, a choice increasingly subject to planned limitation and control. Advertising, 'once the local absurdity of puffing, is now a system of mimed celebration of other people's decisions'. And Raymond Williams goes on:

> An out-dated and inefficient kind of information about goods and services has been surpassed by the competitive needs of the corporations, and these increasingly demand not a sector but a world, not a reservation but a whole society, not a break or a column but whole newspapers and broadcasting services in which to operate.*

Or, as McLuhan more tersely puts it, 'The world of business has taken on the character of Show Business'.

This was not of course just one of the abuses of what progressives hopefully called Late Capitalism. It was equally a feature of the 'socialist' societies. In both worlds, the demands of mass production called the tune. 'The impression, say, of a casual observer in the US watching an endless stream of twenty-ton trucks hurtling through the night, from East to West and from West to East, is that here, indeed, are the visible manifestations of economic power and prosperity. The freight, however, ranges from dish-washing machines to electronic bugging devices, from electric tooth brushes to plastic baubles, and from cosmetics to frozen television suppers.'†

As mass production escalated, so did waste and refuse. Indestructible plastic containers replaced perishable paper and cardboard and the throw-away bottle or can replaced the returnable, multiplying many times over the difficulties of the local authorities and

* R. Williams, writing in *The Listener* (31 July 1969).
† Edward J. Mishan, 'The Spillover Enemy', *Encounter* (December 1969).

of the gallant ladies of the Keep Britain Tidy group. Planned obsolescence and trivial styling changes stepped up the turnover in consumer durables and the intake of the car wreckers. Farms which had for centuries been minor miracles of multiple use and reuse became junkheaps, and blue polythene fertiliser bags blew about the fields. The most brilliant technology of all was predictably the most wasteful, and the earth now spun eternally in its own refuse heap of discarded ironmongery.

All these prodigal habits and the pointlessness of thrift and good housekeeping in a chronically insecure and inflationary world are reflected in the humiliating contrast between the old and the new parts of towns.

Like an old tool, the old town is worn by use into a subtle embodiment and projection of human activity. Its stones and setts are polished by wear instead of pot-holed, and gleam like marble. Its forms are eroded as if by wind or water which hate the acute angle and the sharp arris. In every crevice, people and animals and plants establish themselves in a rough symbiosis. Roofs and walls, patched and stitched like an old shirt, show the scars of their long war with damp like maps of unknown continents. Generations of graffiti and extinct proclamations adorn the accessible parts. Scores of layers of paint round off the edges of cornices and window frames. Brick and stone is left shadowed and highlighted by time, or at random washed down, repainted or repointed. Stucco is madly distempered, then left to fade back. Pipes and wires loop about like failed experiments. Statues are put up or removed, churches restored or ignored. The absurd or handsome streets and spaces and dangerous junctions, the despair of the borough engineer, are in sight of a costly but decisive victory over motor traffic.

The new parts are much more extensive, of course, and more prolific, often shooting seeds of change in the form of new set-back concrete structures into the heart of the old. Some of the older suburbs will already have been reabsorbed by the growth of trees into relationship with the organic world. But on the whole the scene is meaningless, like a confused battle for some cause in which nobody believes. Boulevards, some of whose trees have failed, are too narrow for traffic, too wide for pedestrians, and end in traffic islands which are planted with a few shrubs that nobody can approach. Commercial buildings of various heights, one or two perhaps skyscrapers, are lined up on each side, except where the odd old house juts forward, irremovable for some obscure legal reason. Puddled alleys run back into a vast wasteland part unused. There is a large dusty or tarmac (depending on the latitude) space where the buses stop and start, with a few garages and the noisiest cafés in town. Harshly lighted radial roads, traditionally formless, with an unnecessary number of gas stations, run out into the corrupted countryside, where among the orchards the engineer's standard curbs are laid out on standard widths and radii, awaiting customers. In many countries, large parts of the new town belong to the municipality, whose housing has that unmistakable air of regimentation, minimum maintenance and casual damage which even the best-conducted local governments seem unable to overcome.

Whereas the old town will have been designed and built by craftsmen, most of this new development will have been designed by architects, and all of it influenced by them. There is no alibi.

Grau, teurer Freund, ist alle Theorie, Und grün des Lebens goldner Baum *

wrote Goethe, and everybody has always agreed. But here it seems to be the other way round. For a hundred years theory has sprung green and prolific from a succession of brilliant minds. But practice seems to get harder instead of easier. It is hardly surprising that voices should be heard writing off the whole neotechnic adventure.

As always when Science is applied to a craft which deals in living organisms, the object of the research, albeit not confessed in so many words, must be to discover and standardise practices yielding as nearly as possible a result on a level with that obtained by those empiricists, more numerous in the past than now, whose work is superlative, but

---

* All theory, dear friend, is grey, but the tree of life is green. (Spoken by Mephistopheles, who 'had all the best lines'.)

whose methods cannot be generalised because they depend on an incommunicable quality of judgement.

Edward Hyams is writing about cider-making, but the 'crafts which deal in living organisms' are a huge unbreakable spectrum that stretches all the way from politics to medicine. The escape from the waste land, if it is to be found, will need to be plotted on a dozen routes at once. But it will not be easy to break out. Of the hardness of that soft word 'conservation' Hannah Arendt is in no doubt:

Under modern conditions, not destruction but conservation spells ruin, because the very durability of conserved objects is the greatest impediment to the turnover process, whose constant gain in speed is the only constancy left wherever it has taken hold.*

* Hannah Arendt, *The Human Condition* (1958).

6

Ends

The genius and the masterpiece can look after themselves.
What we should be concerned with are aptness, tact and
efficiency.

John Berger

At this low point we may usefully sum up the argument of the
book so far.

From the beginning, architecture has been the child of two
parents, which I have called Parameters and Images. Unfortunately
for this metaphor, we cannot call them the male and the female
principle, since we have noted that the parameters are by no
means all mechanical or technical: some of them are wholly
earthy in a very 'female' sort of way and have been expressed in
earth-structures wholly female in form. Conversely, the imagery
which has obsessed the mind of the architect has by no means been
all emotional or archetypal: some of it has been highly intellectual
and abstract, and has been expressed in structures as cool as a
mathematical equation. The only safe generalisation is that historically architects have paid much less attention to the parameters
than they should have and supposed they had, and been much
more beguiled by a much more complex set of images than they
would have acknowledged.

All the same, at rare intervals, it has been recognised that the
jungle of imagery was getting out of hand, and then a purge
analogous to similar movements in politics has been prescribed.
Most of these attempts, like Burlington's or Soane's or William

Morris's, turned out, as in politics, to be nothing more than the substitution of a decent image for a decadent one. The only revolution which has seriously persisted in the attempt to stamp out imagery and work purely from the parameters is the modern one of the last hundred years. This persistence was the achievement not of the great iconoclasts, whom we have seen creating new images as busily as they destroyed the old ones, but of their anonymous followers of the second generation, mainly in England.

But when the people of this persuasion tried to push their philosophy up to the scale of cities and landscape we saw them run into trouble. For one thing, they were up against the historical fact that no architect working at city scale had ever, except on paper, completed his project. Townscape and landscape were a process, not a product: time, not technics, was its master parameter. This was why the Baroque aesthetic, the first attempt to embrace town and country in a single gesture, and the Georgian town, the first attempt to apply humanism and rationality to housing, both went down before the Victorian explosion of wealth and population. And this was why the planning theories of the 1950s were so ill-equipped to resist the counter-revolutionary onslaught of the 1960s. Evidently they were too simple to stand up to the facts of life.

So we have seen a sudden, unpredicted loss of confidence in a movement which had seemed more deeply founded than any before in hard thought, social conscience and technical know-how, not to mention superb public presentation. This has been no intramural aesthetes' punch-up of the kind that had grown familiar in the eighteenth and nineteenth centuries, before the days of mass concern in such matters. The remarkable thing about the disenchantment of the 1960s has been an uneasy but effective working alliance between the *avant-garde*, the aesthetic backwoodsmen and the non-visual consumer in the street. Welfare State planning and architecture, like political liberalism, has found itself under attack from all points of the compass.

The unpopularity of modern architecture and planning is a

novel phenomenon confined to a few western countries in a few recent decades. There is no evidence of its existence in the communist countries or the 'developing' ones, where on the whole the opposite is the case: pride or envy, according to circumstances, seem to be the rule. And equally there is no historical evidence of this kind of general dislike of the style of one's own period. Even the Victorians, with the exception of the little band of desperate seers, were perfectly content with the work of their worst architects: the only thing that bothered respectable society was the work of their best engineers. The slums of course were another matter: they were a social problem, not an architectural one. Earlier ages, *a fortiori*, had still less to worry about: to them every new speculation marked the onward march of civilisation. Of 'unspoilt' landscape there was enough and to spare.

Of course our shortage of this in western Europe partly explains our generalised dislike of bricks and mortar. But it goes wider and deeper. We hate not only what the builders are doing in the country but what the architects are doing in the towns. We hate civic centres and shopping precincts and car parks and the absence of car parks. We dread highway improvements and landscaping, public conveniences and public sculpture and municipal murals. London, with its set of uniquely dingy railway termini, hates its only clean one; Paris hates its office blocks; Rome hates its flats; New York prefers its obsolete skyscrapers to its new ones. We object to the low density and lack of privacy of suburban housing and to the high density and loneliness of urban, and we show with pride the dwindling and often unusable by-gones of past squalor and cupidity, rather than the achievements of the most productive and socially oriented generation of architects in history.

It is worth trying to dissect this movement of disenchantment into its component parts. On its right is the perennial reaction against technological and social change, Ruskinian nostalgia for the eotechnic world, die-hard attribution of modernism to foreigners, intellectuals, Jews, socialists and *nouveaux riches:* not strictly disenchantment since these people were never for an instant enchanted. They are the hardcore conservatives that are always at hand, reaching out for the pendulum of change when at regular intervals it swings their way, but never able to grasp it. We have to accept the fact that we are in for one of their 'I told you so' phases. Then in the centre are the Poujadists, persistently barking at the heels of the Big Battalions. Their enemies are the multiple stores, the multi-storey flats, the multilevel garages, and all the takeovers that threaten what they have been taught to call the 'quality of life'. Allied to them but more sophisticated are those individualists – artists in the mould of Piper and Wyeth, novelists in the mould of Orwell, poets in the mould of Larkin and Betjeman – who see in every overworked, worried planning officer a little Big Brother and our world firmly on its way to 1984. The architect's image in contemporary literature has been bad for a long time: he has been rated as a humourless idealist, blissfully unaware of the realities of life.

Well to the left of these liberals is the new generation of pop architects, LSE sociologists and mannerist critics whose role is to undermine the conventional wisdom from inside. Their attack is essentially against the crudely generalised dogmatic assertions of the modern establishment, masquerading as works of high art, their aim, in Venturi's words, to 'awaken architects from prim dreams of pure order', or in those of D.H.Lawrence (always a safe guide to this line of thought):

> It's bad taste to be wise all the time,
>   like being at a perpetual funeral.
> For everyday use, give me somebody whimsical,
>   with not too much purpose in life:
> Then we shan't have war,
>   and we needn't talk about peace.

Finally, and conversely, out on the fringes, are the initiates of communications theory and cybernetics, experts in that old game of discrediting current thought structures by inventing a secret language that excludes them, while busily assembling new structures that will be equally inadequate and immature.

Superficially one could write off a good deal of this as mere fashion on the same level as Pugin's remark on returning from a visit to a friend at Oxford: 'how strange to find such a glorious man as Ward living in a room without mullions!' We know from history that it is by violent and inherently absurd reactions like this that aesthetic thought develops and art stays alive – unlike technology, which develops structurally, each generation standing on the shoulders of the one before. But the present reaction is too wide a spectrum to be frivolously dismissed; it would be more profitable to look for what is serious about it rather than what is comic, and particularly to see whether there is a single thread running through it all.

And of course there is, though it is sometimes wrongly identified because it can be approached from opposite directions. In other words there are some who find our style too intellectual, too austerely cerebral, too self-conscious, too clever, and others who find it too slap-dash, too easy to do, too emotionally impoverished and in fact too stupid. Either way, the missing characteristics are the same: warmth, care, spontaneity, diversity. It has lost, both parties would agree, its human face, and so become suddenly, alarmingly irrelevant.

> They've tried to grasp with too much social fact
> Too large a situation. You and I
> Would be afraid if we should comprehend
> And get outside of too much bad statistics
> Our muscles never could again contract:
> We never could recover human shape.

Robert Frost here speaks for the extreme right, but here is Peter Cook, a generation later, finding in the Architectural Association Senior Year of 1969 the seeds of change:

> I detect in the work of several students the beginnings of a vitality that had signs of drying out in the face of so much solid reading and reluctance to act without fact ... certainly at all levels of the AA School there is a proliferation of studies into piecemeal redevelopment, rehabilitation and Do-It-Yourself.*

One can sense and share from one's own experience the feeling of

* Peter Cook, in the *AA Quarterly* (Autumn 1969).

relief at the possibility of escape from the hard living and high thinking, from the pursuit of regressive facts that could never be wholly mastered, from the obligation to produce a serious contribution to the Modern Movement, that life with the parameters involved for us all. Attendance at that 'perpetual funeral' was not much fun either for producers or consumers. Architects habitually envy the relaxed will of the 'pure' artist and strain at the yoke of Science to which they submitted for life when they decided to design buildings. The question is whether this reaction is mere exhaustion of the kind which weakened Gothic architecture in the fourteenth century and Renaissance architecture in the sixteenth. If we descend from Parnassus do we get lost in the jungle of the world?

We must face the fact that until now architecture has always been part of a consistent and credible view of the world, whether it was the Vitruvian mix of lucky science and superstition, or the great allegories of the cathedrals, or the Newtonian clockwork universe under the watchful eye of a beneficent Creator. It was precisely because architecture seemed to have lapsed, under Romantic stresses, from this position of centrality that the Victorians set out on that long struggle to reinstate it on which the Bauhaus seemed to have set its seal. At about the mid-point of this century, in a world chastened by war and not yet aroused to the inadequacies of peace, it really did seem that we had the answer to the question asked at the inaugural meeting of the Architectural Association a hundred years before: 'the great question is, are we to have an architecture of our period, a distinct, individual, palpable style of the nineteenth century?'

The man who asked this question had more on his mind than keeping up with the Jones's of the past. His generation was adrift in the interregnum between Newton and Einstein, in the gulf between religion and science. They knew, as we know as soon as we try it, that the human mind has to operate within a structure of some kind: it needs points of reference to give it direction, scale, balance, time-sense, let alone the criteria by which it forms value-judgements. Remove objective and conscious landmarks and we at once set up subjective and subconscious ones. A merely *ad hoc*, makeshift architecture is literally inconceivable.

Fortunately we have our node, our pole-star, a very small star, but more tactile, more objectively and lucidly *there* than ever before in human history – that sapphire and diamond globe that we have photographed from the blackness of space and on which we now know that we sail alone in our solar system. Our aesthetic sense, which makes the moon look so drab and meaningless under its blinding arc-lamp, was earth-born and earth-bred. We call a thing beautiful because we find the earth so, and because it goes well with the earth. Our sense of beauty (if the word is still permissible) is nothing more than a sense of ease of the kind into which we relax when a group of people go well together. It does not have to be analysed. But it does have to be cultivated: we need to feel deeply ashamed when we hurt the earth, as Nietzsche in one of his prophetic insights foresaw:

> Once the sin against God was the greatest sin; but God died and those sinners died with him. To sin against the earth is now the most dreadful thing.*

Let us try this philosophy for size. What are its implications?

First, silence. The globe upon which men developed and succeeded was silent. Every sound made a mark on this silence and had a meaning. Noise is meaningless sound, so that as it becomes noisier, the world becomes less meaningful. Already in the 'developed' countries a fine day is never silent: aircraft, hovercraft, road and rail traffic, farm machinery, heating and ventilating plant, refrigerators, musak, between them fill the gaps and overlap. So sounds have to make what mark they can not on a white surface, but on a dark one; and they have to compete with superimposed unwilled noises like the agonising acceleration of heavy lorries and motorcycles, the scream of brakes, the racket of compressors. In the inflating spiral nobody can speak or sing without a microphone and the rousing bell of the London fire engine has to be replaced by an unnerving siren of ten times the power. To win

* Nietzsche, 'Thus Spake Zarathustra' (1883).

through, youth makes its mark on this distracted world by means of the pop group's amplifiers which can break your eardrums if you go too close. We have reached the point where silence has switched from negative to positive and become one of the great luxuries.

The same goes for clean air and clear water, taken for granted for millennia. 'Happiness,' said Logan Pearsall Smith, 'is a wine of the rarest vintage and seems insipid to a vulgar taste.' So do those other best things in life which used to be said to be free, but unobtainable. So do clean air and clear water. One soon ceases to notice the taste of different waters, or prefers a Coca-Cola to any, just as one soon prefers a chlorinated pool to the Mediterranean, motor to sail, a televised event to a real one. The trouble is that this slide once started accelerates; yet sooner or later it has to be stopped. When seven million tons of coal dust fall on Pittsburgh in a single year and all the fish in the Rhine die in a single day, something very difficult and expensive has to be done. In the worst polluted countries we have at last begun to feel the necessary sense of guilt: the burden has begun to shift from the social to the moral account where we feel it more. Already in London a smoking chimney makes us feel uncomfortable and a filthy exhaust makes us look for a policeman. Before long no doubt a pang of guilt will strike at the instant we drop the cigarette packet or the beer can, and the captain who releases an oil slick will be haunted like a murderer.

The other planets are all desert or worse. Our climatic cycle is the only one we know of which through millennia has created and can still create the infinitesimally thin membrane of topsoil on which all terrestrial life depends. Every action which diminishes it diminishes us. If it is true, as has been said, that the world takes for development the area of an English county every *day*, then we have less than a century to go before we have consumed the whole of its cultivable land. So waste of this land is a crime against humanity: every windbreak effective against erosion that is felled and ploughed up to raise farm income, every steep slope cleared of the timber that grappled the soil to the rocks beneath, every slap-dash *lotissement* that leaves odd corners unusable, every shrubbed-up SLOIP* in every pretentious city centre, is professional negligence in some profession that holds our future in its hands. We should get so that it hurts to see some small plants denied life by a lump of concrete left in the undergrowth. This may seem precious, but so is the material we are concerned with.

As for trees, we may recognise them as a paradigm of ourselves, with their roots in the earth and their head in the clouds, but for centuries we have used them to show off our power to grow something so much taller than ourselves, and then our power in a few moments to bring it down. In between, trees can be stunted, pruned, pleached, laid and lopped. They are a means by which people have expressed themselves, either in prim ranks demonstrating Divine Order, or as bleached skeletons, commemorating the pioneer spirit of dead colonists, or in bosky groves displaying the refinement of the Augustan Age. Only recently have we learnt to let them be what they want to be by applying to them the principles of resource management, using neither brutality nor sentimentality. But we are still too blind to see that there is something wrong with the values of a culture which takes 150 acres of virgin forest to produce a single Sunday issue of the *New York Times*, or else too lazy to do anything about it.

With animals our relationship is different, stemming from a different past. They are a subject race, living in fear or sycophancy. For them it is purely the luck of the draw whether they are exterminated as pests, cossetted as pets, bred and fattened for slaughter or granted a precarious apartheid subject to periodic cullings to maintain our balance of nature – not theirs, which might have worked better. Too much history lies between us and them for us ever again to go out and lie down with them as Whitman wanted. All we can hope for, and of course we have begun to work towards it, is a more intelligent symbiosis than the help-yourself exploitation of the past. Already our relationship has begun to change, or perhaps revert, from mere greed to a kind of envy.

* Space Left Over In Planning.

How is it that human beings will submit to the gyps of previous history while mere creatures look with their original eyes?

Saul Bellow here touches on the mystery which haunted the palaeolithic artists, to whom the slain beast was so much grander than the little matchstick men who did the killing. Any philosophy of conservation has to live with the primeval paradox, as old as our departure from the Garden of Eden, that most of our fellow-passengers on the planet live by preying on one another, exemplifying a mutual dependence that transcends the individual.

Reinhold Niebuhr extended the paradox into a dilemma, writing in the middle of a war which exemplified it, that 'Goodness armed with power is corrupted, and pure love without power is destroyed'. We shall not possess the beginnings of a philosophy on which an architecture could be built unless we can reach the depths of this truth and learn to live with it. To love the blue and white planet, to learn to pass through it as harmlessly as an elephant slips through a bamboo forest, not breaking a twig, none of this is enough. We cannot, like Keats, 'open our hearts like a flower and be passive and receptive'. For we are the bees of this world, not the flowers, and we have to be busy about its dilemmas. For example it is distressingly plain that all our environmental problems – noise, congestion, erosion, pollution, exploitation, waste – come back to one problem: population. Yet to *act* on this urgent fact needs decisions of a kind so dreary, negative, and anti-life that we shrink from taking them: we shrink from arming love with power. But we are going to have to do it.

If we translate Niebuhr's dilemma into terms more clearly related to the world of architecture, if for love we read conservation in its broadest sense, and for power we read change in its toughest, we perhaps begin to see the shape of the territory within which a relevant architecture will need to operate.

We can now return to the question of what went wrong with the modern movement and weakened its powers of resistance to the inevitable reaction. We have seen that it was an unprecedently synthetic and self-conscious movement. It began with the search for a New Architecture, capable of turning its back on 'dead styles'. It was thought that the best source of new ideas must be the 'new' materials, steel, reinforced concrete, plate-glass, rather than the 'old' ones, stone, clay products, forest products. It was thought that 'ornament', unless hand-wrought, was immoral, and that the tastes and desires of the man in the street were vulgar and degrading. Futurism put forward a set of values based on western middle-class tastes for mechanics, electronics, speed and sunbathing that were more or less irrelevant to the great masses of humanity. The Bauhaus produced beautiful individual works of art, but its understanding of industrial processes was amateurish and its lines of communication with the outside world obscure and precarious. Even the more down-to-earth British school worked in an ideological vacuum and made no visible impact on a society which prefers to fly salesmen at Mach 2·5 than to give everybody somewhere to live.

We had in fact a difficult, highbrow architecture which lacked centrality in its ambient culture, an architects' architecture which had failed (even when it tried) to establish communications with society either as it is or as it ought to be. Hence the attack on two fronts, to each of which it inevitably presented an image of puritanism, arrogance and defensiveness.

The test of this is when you visit a strange city and ask a local architect to show you the new modern work. You mention the forests of tower cranes visible from your hotel window, the whole quarters demolished and rebuilt since the war. 'Oh no, not that, not that!' your shocked host cries. And off you go in his car through acres of new townscape from which he hopes you will avert your eyes, through miles of new suburbia, to find the small primary school, or the house, or the branch library, which he thinks sufficiently decent for you to see. Nothing could be more literally eccentric. The place as a whole, as an environment, as an expression of our culture, is clearly in this man's opinion somebody else's affair, or nobody's. As for the overloaded planet, the ravaged resources, the upset balances, the lost images, these night thoughts clearly have nothing to do with architecture.

This is all very Victorian and understandable. All through that age the architect had been an aloof and uncommunicative aesthete speaking an esoteric professional language. The trouble is that it was precisely this alienation from society which the reformers aimed to break down. They repeatedly said so. Gropius spoke of

an ever wider and profounder conception of design as one great cognate whole – the mirror of the indivisibility and immensity and underlying unity of life itself, of which it is an integral part.*

Lethaby wrote that he didn't believe in genius one bit, nor anything else abnormal. He 'wanted the commonplace'. 'Art should be everywhere. It cannot exist in isolation or one-man-thick; it must be a thousand men thick.' And in a statement to which the whole modern movement would have subscribed:

It is impossible to draw any line giving architecture a superior status to building that does not result in defining it in such a way as may leave some of the best and most beautiful buildings in the 'non' class while retaining some of the most dreadful ones within the fold. . . . It is only by bettering the whole body of building that we shall be able to raise the summit.†

Both Lethaby and Gropius, brought up in the Arts-and-Crafts tradition, and even Herbert Read in a later generation, could see no way to achieve this except in the dissemination of creative work as part of the educational process. You must learn by doing.

Old customary art was a tenderness of mind given to the hard-handed: now art is soft-handed but hard-hearted.†

Unfortunately, as the building industry became progressively more automated this doctrine became progressively more irrelevant to it. Nevertheless the reformers continued to preach it. As late as 1939, Wright could still speak of 'the end of architecture and of all art as some fashionable aesthetic' and of 'an organic architecture, the architecture of Democracy', forgetting his own manifestly aristocratic nature and the fact that nearly all his clients were millionaires, and forgetting, more seriously, that the democ-

* Walter Gropius, *The New Architecture and the Bauhaus* (1935).
† W.R.Lethaby, *Scrips and Scraps*, ed. A.H.Powell (1956).

racy he referred to was an urbanised mass, split down the middle racially, and confined for its working hours at least to the most elaborately mechanised and inorganic environments in human history. Le Corbusier, with his much more vivid awareness of the size of the problem, offered solutions *de haut en bas* in the French intellectual tradition. Too sophisticated to believe in a grass-roots architecture, he plumped instead for the abstract Germanic notion of the epoch's irresistible Will to Form as manifested in the un-selfconscious work of the engineers. Here again, as the common factor in the philosophies of all the reformers, we have the deep suspicion of conventional capital-A architecture and the hope that a new spirit would rise phoenix-like from the bonfire. When it failed, he turned unashamedly to an aestheticism of a wholly personal kind.

What none of the pioneers seem to have noticed was the contradiction between their demotic aims and their refined aesthetics. No puritanical movement can ever be popular. Imagery is fun, and history has never had a kind word to say for the Roundhead troops who smashed our medieval sculpture and stained glass. Iconoclasm on high can equal vandalism in the streets. We can now see that while our architectural iconoclasm was probably necessary in the conditions of the time, it could never be final: the long fight to convert a destructive into a creative force could not be won on that narrow front. For those styles and that ornament, which superficially seemed and often were a silly sort of fancy dress, could also have much deeper reverberations, and there was no geigercounter, and never could be, by which you could identify the archetypal images in the old lumber room. So you put a match to the whole lot. As a result, the whole movement like an inverted pyramid balanced on too narrow an emotional base.

It was also of course, and was so described by its left-wing enemies, a bourgeois movement. The assumptions that architecture is an art, that art must always be an elitist activity, that ordinary people cannot be trusted to make judgements about it, go back to Plato and are so deeply rooted in the European psyche that it never occurred to the movement to think seriously about the implications of treating itself as something different – like politics, the art of love and free discussion, all of which were regarded as elitist activities through most of history and have only recently been opened up. It was all talk.

In all these ways the modern movement, like most others, can be made to look more like an end than a beginning. This obviously does not mean writing it off and starting again. That would be to repeat its own mistake. When you get stuck on a climb, you do not go back to the bottom. You relax and then call on such reserves of moral energy as you possess. Otherwise you have no hope of holding the gains you have made. The question is whether the set of attitudes to our world that I have described in this chapter, by broadening the base of architecture both philosophically and socially, could be the foundation of a better relationship between the architect and society. The best way of answering it is to imagine a set-up in which these attitudes have the authority without which they are valueless. This we must now do.

7

Beginnings

Nature rambles and a few periods of visual appreciation at primary school are not much of a start on this huge task of reintegration. You need more than a bus ride out of Birmingham before you will make contact with a world most English children were torn out of a century and a half ago. We start, in fact, with a vicious circle: how can we possibly expect people to like the world better until it is more likeable, and how will it be made likeable if nobody cares for it? One can only say that all movements of conversion start in this circle and have to break out; for which they need, first, a vision.

There have been two moments in history when the beauty and drama of the physical world struck humanity like a revelation, and both were moments of escape from structured universes with rigidly conventional ways of seeing. The first was the escape from the blinkered medieval world and the second was the escape from the Age of Reason. Both the Renaissance and the Romantic movement, after the shock of exhilaration had passed, were characterised by a passionate exploration of the detail of the newly revealed world. It was as though one had landed on a new star.

Is it conceivable that our jaded appetites, which have experienced by proxy all that the world has to offer and have even been deluded into dreaming that there are better worlds elsewhere, could be coaxed back to these familiar pastures? I think it highly likely that it is. Many signs point that way. There is the recoil from the technological Utopia, which makes a great deal more historical

sense than its apparent economic nonsense may suggest. There is
the retreat from abstraction and the group of movements in the
arts which enjoy the visual accidents thrown up by the world as
it is. There is the surge in the numbers of people who can get out
of the conurbations: the queues for the rock-climbs, the long wait
for yacht moorings, the multifold increase in the numbers of
spare-time naturalists, archaeologists, and mere sightseers. Above
all there is the growing sense of how precious the 'unspoilt' world
is: its simple scarcity value right now, let alone in the inescapable
future.

> How sweet I roamed from field to field
> And tasted all the summer's pride.

Blake's words have a new poignancy, because we know how rare
those flowers are, how rare to hear nothing in the sky but larks.

Whether from these crude beginnings this nation, or others
equally brutalised by nineteenth-century industrialism or twentieth-century gadgetry, could build a universal love of the world
in Nietzsche's sense is another matter. Could these goggling
strangers in the inherited world learn to feel for it an animal em-
pathy, catch the rhythms of growth and change, welcome the
limits of the weather and the seasons, lie on the ground and feel
the world turning? No good sending for the Secretary of State
for Education and Science, or the police. The kiss of death by
which Western societies have learnt to absorb revolutionary movements had better not be proffered here, because this would turn
a change of heart, which is communicated by contagion, into a
change of policy, communicated by instruction. In no time it
could have become a new kind of censorship, or a neutered hour
of quasi-religious platitude, water off a duck's back. This movement will prosper among the Antigones of this world, not the
Creons.

We are not speaking of a 'back-to-nature' movement. Blake's
fields were man-made, or it would have been no sweet roam: he
would have been fighting his way through thorn and bramble.
Nor is this a matter of aesthetics in the conventional sense. It is a

matter of understanding, of the kind of affection people feel for their families with their familiar faults and for their homes with their tiresome snags. Wonder and terror were in order when the world was young and most of it undiscovered. Now we may still be scared to death by the sea or the mountains or the things that can go wrong in the air, but we feel we have the measure of our planet. We understand the forces that shaped its surface, we can picture from the air the organic relationship between village and landscape in India, we enjoy the slate quarries of North Wales as much as the waterfalls, preserve in a museum the foyer of the Strand Palace Hotel as well as the Great Bed of Ware, admire our Victorian cities as much as our medieval ones. Having lived through so much more history, we live in a visually far richer world.

For example in the last ten years there has been an extraordinary change of feeling about old towns. To the modernists of the 1920s, as we have seen, old towns were old junk – a kind of bricky scrub in which the new architecture was to plant its bright saplings of renewal, or which it might be necessary to scrape away wholesale, as Le Corbusier proposed to do in his *Plan Voisin* for central Paris. It is very easy to fall into this arrogant contempt for old buildings. Like old people, they can be squalid, expensive to maintain and awkward to convert. Unflattering photographs can be taken of their much-abused backs, cracked parapets and comic necklaces of pipework. But a time comes – came in England in the early 1960s – when you face the surprise that it is not so easy to do better. We only had to experience a few brand-new developers' shopping centres to discover overnight that we preferred what had been there before, scruffy though it was. Then a new factor supervened. Narrow old streets, hitherto treated as traffic bottle-necks and spasmodically widened, could by new and bolder traffic planning be wholly freed of vehicles and revert to their medieval pedestrian use. Footfalls could be heard again, and people laughing. And of course in the new peace and quiet it became possible to think of living in the place again. Upper floors that had stood empty for generations invited conversion into flats at what could even be economic rents. The old town suddenly worked.

Civic and amenity societies, hitherto the preserve of tiny groups of professional people, proliferated all over Europe and grew like beanstalks. The old rule that only old people worried about old buildings ceased to apply, and students volunteered in droves to record them, convert them and inhabit them. Street facelifts, first tried by the Civic Trust in Norwich, became fashionable among dons and spread to unsuitable places like the golden medieval streets of Oxford. Councillors in traditionally philistine northern cities found themselves blown along by winds of conservation instead of change. Packed public meetings volunteered to pay higher rates to help save the old streets. The thing was getting out of hand.

Nor was it only the recognised beauty spots that came into their own. The Cities of Dreadful Night, the scenes fastidiously by-passed by persons of taste on their way to Scotland, the Lake District or North Wales, began to build up their supporters' clubs. Liverpool became a cult, Glasgow achieved recognition as the grandest of Victorian cities. Manchester, Newcastle, Bradford and Bristol no sooner got into their stride with slum clearance than they ran into trouble with preservationists. In Britain Ian Nairn and in America Jane Jacobs, significantly neither of them architects, put in their diversionary attacks on the conventional wisdom. Much of all this was a rag, cocking a snook at the headmaster on the first day of the holidays. Much of it was simply the artist's affectionate curiosity about things as they are, given new scope and *chic* by the discoveries of pop art. Constable is supposed to have said that he had never seen an ugly thing in his life, and of course if you went all the way with that attractive philosophy you shirked all judgement and abandoned yourself to enjoying the soft-drinks stall below the waterfall. You licked the boots of the vandal.

If we go back half a century we find a proper balance in a letter written from India by Patrick Geddes, in which he admits how he has been

tempted, like an impatient chess-player, to sweep a fist through the pieces which stand in the way. This destructive impatience is, indeed, an old vice of beginners in positions of authority; and their chance of learning the real game is, of course, spoiled by such an abuse of it.*

The 'real game' had turned out much harder to learn than Geddes or any of its other originators anticipated, and this is why its professional players, all honourable men, have suffered the indignity of being jeered and booed by the crowd. But we can take heart from the fact that the stands are empty no longer. As when one late afternoon a dramatic match approaches its climax at Wimbledon people are drawn to it from other courts, conscious that it is here that the future is being made.

The first thing that the professionals have to learn is a common language. Even among architects, who are by no means the only people concerned, this does not yet exist. Anyone who has taken part in a planning inquiry will know that each side, taking diametrically opposite views, will have little trouble in securing its 'expert witness'. So there are raised eyebrows at this word 'expert', which is regarded by laymen as a courtesy title given to persons who practise an art in which *de gustibus non disputandum*. They are wrong. Values exist, but some architects have been brought up to give them absolute authority, others to regard their client's interest (like that of a doctor's patient) as paramount, others have not been brought up at all, but have developed the cynicism of bitter experience. Even more unbridgeable gulfs of misunderstanding separate architects from their colleagues in the building/planning team – from builders themselves, who are tied into market economics and whose business is to make money out of bricks and mortar, from engineers, whose training conditions them to solve problems not to ask whether they should have been set, from surveyors of all kinds, whose concern is with the marshalling of facts, not decision-making, and even from planners, the staff officers who set up the battle but do not have to fight in it. The result is an uneasy, *ad hoc* coalition between little nations whose backgrounds and casts-of-mind are hopelessly at variance.

The basis of the missing language should by now be clear. It

* Patrick Geddes, *Letters from India* (1947).

is that the safety of the ship comes first for the very good reason that the crew's lives depend on it. But the analogy is inadequate because this space-ship of ours has to be continually modified as the voyage proceeds. So Conservation is too narrow, because we are concerned with development, and Doxiadis's word Ekistics is too narrow because we are concerned with conservation. If the discipline needs a Greek word it can only be Geosophy: the wisdom of the world. Like any discipline, it is a kind of code so built into one's thought processes that reference to it is unconscious. The essence of it is to put the whole before the part, to see our own activity, whatever its scale, as modifying a totality rather than as self-sufficient in itself. Applied objectively to any project we need to assess, it is to take the frame away and see the picture as part of the room. It is akin to the lucidity and detachment which the French encyclopaedists sought to apply to every question, except that they set their sights too high, attempted a universality that could not be sustained, and lost the viable parts in their loss of the whole. More relevant, curiously enough, is John Ruskin with his code of 'submission', which for a century made him a figure of fun in the mythology of the modern movement. Yet now, in the last volume of *Modern Painters*, he seems to speak directly of our situation:

And I desire, especially, that the reader should note this, in now closing the work through which we have passed together in the investigation of the beauty of the visible world. For perhaps he expected more pleasure and freedom in that work; he thought that it would lead him at once into fields of fond imagination, and may have been surprised to find that the following of beauty brought him always under a sterner dominion of mysterious law; that brightness was continuously based upon obedience, and all majesty only another form of submission. But this is indeed so. I have been perpetually hindered in this enquiry into the sources of beauty by fear of wearying the reader with their severities. It was always accuracy I had to ask of him, not sympathy; patience, not zeal; apprehension, not sensation. The thing to be shown him was not a pleasure to be snatched, but a law to be learned.

Obviously in an elementary sense we are concerned simply with an attitude of mind, and traditionally, as with conventional religion, or Marxism, or the American Way of Life, you cultivate this in young children in the home or the primary school. So signally has all such indoctrination failed in our time that it could well be best to leave this kind of love, like all others, within the lore of Protest, so that a whole generation can claim it as its own. But when it comes to the professionals, to the planners, architects, engineers, etc. whose recent adventures of the spirit this book has tried to record, there can be no doubt at all that if this is to be their common language, it has to be communicated. No doubt a joint university first year is necessary. Gropius saw the same necessity, but his Bauhaus *Vorkurs* was dedicated to creativity whereas ours would be dedicated to understanding. In the then state of art-instruction in the schools, his first-year students had to start by un-learning; ours would be building on a sense of mission without which they would not be there at all.

In this first year the over-riding necessity to protect the bio-sphere would be established in the first term, the sense of its past and of its rhythms of change in the second, and some examples of current dilemmas confronted in the third. One would emerge with a sense of crisis, a sense of scale and a sense of responsibility – no more – and individual temperament and public need would decide whether one went on into government or design or construction or farming or ecology. Within the field of planning and building the present carve-up into trades and professions is rooted in Victorian society, in which the architect was literate, the engineer and surveyor numerate and the contractor neither. The architect dealt in ideas, the engineer in solutions, the builder in men. If all were grounded together in our first year, one would expect these distinctions to fade. One would expect the architect to go into construction, the builder to worry about the social context, and the technical supporting arms to be as deeply concerned as anybody else with the strategy. Increasingly, as the assembly of buildings needs the skills of a cybernetician rather than a sergeant-major, one can see design and construction integrated in one package under the leadership of a man or a group who will certainly want to call themselves architects, but who will be very different from the lonely, vulnerable, gentle figure of the past.

It is these new people we shall mean when we use the word architect in the pages that follow. What they will inherit with the name is the architect's inveterate tendency to question the particular in the cause of the general. Unlike lawyers, who do the opposite, and in this more like doctors, who check on the patient's general state of health before they prescribe a specific remedy, architects will feel ill at ease unless the whole context – or anyway all the parameters – are revealed to them. But unlike doctors, their patient is not their client: their patient is the human environment, or in this particular corner of it, and there will be cases – hard, worrying cases – where they have to tell their client that the environment has a prior claim over his project. 'Supra-client values', as Gurth Higgin has called them, impose on the architect a duty beyond that of acting as his client's agent which is unique to him and which can make him seem arrogant, obstinate or even disloyal. It can't be helped. What endless damage and maltreatment the landscape and townscape could have been saved if this duty had been second nature to architects in the past!

It was not so, not solely for the mundane reason that architects were afraid to lose the job, but more commonly because they lacked the moral 'bottom' of that first year's initiation. They did not feel the wounds of the earth in the right part of their emotional anatomy. The dilemma simply didn't present itself. Or if it did, they repressed it. They blinded themselves to the wrong they were doing and took shelter behind the alibi that if they didn't go ahead and try to make the best of a bad job some other and probably worse architect would be found without the slightest difficulty, and the last state of that project would be worse than the first. If this was true, and it often was, it simply showed that the crime was not an individual but a collective one.

These are of course conservationist arguments, and it is very easy to change a letter or two and misread them as conservative ones – anti-change as such. This would be absurd. Change is the architect's habitat, the air he breathes, the raw material of his industry, and in a thousand ways the environment needs to change more than it needs to stay the same. The argument here is between blind change and seeing change, and our purpose is to get closer to an understanding and definition of the second, since it is in this hazy territory of value judgement that the professional has to operate and has to convince people that he knows his way.

In the early Victorian days of professionalism it was hoped that prestige would do the trick. The architect's financial integrity was assured by forbidding him a direct stake in the sale of sites or materials or buildings. Decently dressed behind the brass plate on his decent front door, a member of the best clubs, the architect's role was to guide and protect his client against the sharks in the building trade. Complications only began to appear when the client turned out a shark himself, and demanded of his architect a hard financial assessment as well as an aesthetic one. Then the Emperor's clothes needed some holding on to: it was no longer quite good enough to cry 'you really must do it this way, even if it costs you more'. Cost-benefit studies were called in aid, and developed with increasing ingenuity in an attempt to put a price-tag on the amenities of life. But they could not always convince, particularly down at the human scale where a little more money could make all the difference between despondency and pleasure. It was much easier to make a case for the new Victoria Line in London than for painting the buses red.

It is precisely because it is so easy to drift rudderless in these seas, blown sideways by conflicting pressures far more powerful than he is himself, that the architect needs the ballast of an altogether larger moral philosophy than the modern movement turned out to be. That which was roughly sketched in the last chapter is I think best given solidity by some examples.

We will take soil conservation as our first. Now we have to face a hard fact – that any loss of cultivable land that is both avoidable and irreversible is in the present state of knowledge a crime against humanity. The main agents of loss are of course buildings, roads and airports. So where we locate them, and the manner in which we build them, have a significance now that they have never had before. This has been almost a platitude for the last twenty years, yet look at the mistakes we have made in this country alone! In a ring round London, in thousands of acres of human-sized fields richly necklaced with mature oak and elm, we have a dozen sprawling new towns at suburban densities which have made only a marginal contribution to the housing of Londoners – no doubt too easy, too inviting to be resisted; and all that industry has been dispersed in penny packets which concentrated in two or three new cities further afield could have trimmed the boat and saved the stores. We have rejected Hook, which was sensibly located on marginal land, in favour of Milton Keynes, which is not. We have let Manchester and Merseyside sprawl even more lazily into the rich soil of their green belts, virtually linked Edinburgh and Glasgow across the fertile waist of Scotland when both had poor hill lands close at hand, let Portsmouth and Southampton spread northwards on to first-class farmland when the one could have built a new Venice in Langstone Harbour and the other commuted from the sandy heaths round Bournemouth. Examples at all scales can be multiplied.

In addition to the use of marginal lands and wet lands, there is in developed countries the huge acreage of spoiled landscapes, of half-urbanised subtopia and abandoned industrial sites – a primary element in the North American scene and a major one in Western Europe. Ian Nairn in 1965 listed fourteen city-size sites on spoiled landscapes in England and Wales, reckoned there were hundreds of smaller ones, and urged that we 'build four-square in the middle of our existing messes' – a nice simple idea, but hard to apply in a democracy, whether the mess be the Swansea valley or the tiny freeholds of Rhyl and Prestatyn.

Moreover of course it is not just a question of dropping so many thousand people into so many hundred hectares of marginal land. For each time one does this, one changes the conditions for the next time: the network acquires new links and changes its total form. And at a deeper level, Lilienthal's seamless web is modified, and ecological effects spread across the island and even across the seas. Take Harry Teggin's hypothesis of a new city in the shallows of the Wash – a city incidentally which complies with our primary condition of taking no farmland whatever except for its road and rail links with the interior. Here the population comes, as it were, last, into a complex geographical-ecological-industrial nest built to receive it: a container-port on the Rotterdam scale directly linking our Midland industries with Europort and by-passing the congestion round London, an offshore airport scaled to inter-continental passengers and freight aircraft, a group of reservoirs impounding the waters of the Witham, Welland, Ouse and Nene, irrigating the dry south-east and supporting new industrial growth, and a substantial addition by further reclamation to the richest silt soil we possess in the British Isles. Cumulative benefits of this kind, on what Teggin describes as the heroic scale, pioneered in the TVA before the war, could have restructured and psycho-logically renewed Britain after it.

But even this scale of thought is inadequate. On the map of the world, no amount of cross-posting within the confines of a tiny island can be very significant. For the British, Australia is con-spicuously the promised land, and nothing less than a national migration of industrial investment and population will meet the case. It is remarkable that no systematic research has been pub-lished in either country into the economics of an operation which on a proper scale could be so obviously in the interests of both.

This overdue leap across the world is a special situation due to a national relationship. More commonly, human settlement creeps across the map like a fungus, along lines of least resistance. Doxiadis in Greece and Gottman in France, in their studies of the mor-phology of urban growth, show how this tends to take a tentacu-lar form along the channels of fast transportation, and that if this is allowed to continue unregulated, cities must inevitably out-grow their central facilities and suffer from the heart disease that has become rampant in the United States. To avoid it, Doxiadis proposes that growth should as far as possible be uni-directional, the centre moving along its own groove parallel with the thrust of the suburbs. Blandly accepting the most fearsome population projections, he sees these powerful streams of urbanised humanity coalescing as irresistibly as the tide invading a sandy estuary, until the whole world has been infiltrated, and the patches of farmland or desert are mere islands in the human sea – a reversal of the traditional relationship of town and country which we can already experience in parts of Britain and America.

Doxiadis would not pretend, and nor should we, that his beguiling diagrams have any aesthetic value at full scale. For whereas the classical city planner from Vitruvius to Le Corbusier created patterns that were intended to be experienced and enjoyed, the contemporary city plan is a diagrammatic armature destined to be buried in distance, with as little visual significance as the map of the London Underground. Perhaps Lucio Costa at Brasilia was the last to attempt, if not to achieve, an intelligible visual entity at the metropolitan scale. Doxiadis' apparently naïve projections do have the great merit of showing how urban growth can and must be given a *direction* if it is not to be blind and destructive, and we can go on to postulate that this direction had better be into marginal land or mountains if mankind is to save up enough soil to keep itself alive.

Compared with possibilities of this order, the space-saving contribution attainable by the internal planning of towns themselves is much less than one might suppose. Roads and car parks must multiply as cars multiply. Office zones are already at densities we can only match by building very high. Recreational space is short already. The only room for manoeuvre is in the design of housing, which is why housing density has been debated *ad nauseam*, particularly in Britain which despite its diminutive land area has always aimed at the highest domestic space standards in the world. For a couple of generations this has been a flats-versus-houses debate, unaffected in principle by tendencies to raise densities in both. Inside the conurbations, with the high proportion of immobile employment, it is inevitable that land redeveloped for mass housing should be at densities only attainable with flats of some sort: otherwise workers would nowadays have to be exiled to impossible commuting distances. The question resolves itself into high-rise versus low-rise flat development – a choice between silence (except for the noise of the wind), great horizons, loneliness, remoteness from ground-level play space, or court-yard echoes, neighbourliness and all the frictions of traditional urban co-existence. All we can do here is to respond as sensitively as possible to both needs and wants.

It is only when we come on to virgin territory that choices significant in terms of land-space are open to us. Here it begins to look as if, in all the crowded countries, the constellations of old settlements, neolithic in origin and confirmed through cen-turies of animal transport, has had its day. The pattern of change is universal: rural depopulation through mechanisation – or despair, a far greater marketing range, and a rush to a small number of multi-million conurbations. In countries with low resources or gross inequalities of wealth, the new arrivals camp round city perimeters in a more or less dramatic posture of siege; in more advanced countries they are absorbed in the old fabric, and the more privileged spread themselves over huge hinter-lands; only in Britain is any serious attempt made to protect the historic pattern of settlement. Our early New Towns, up to and including Cumbernauld, were of course dedicated to this attempt, not only by their comparatively small scale and their greenbelts, but also by the efforts of their planners to 'improve' on the low densities of Letchworth and Welwyn, and achieve a more com-pact and identifiable urban form. Milton Keynes signalises the end of this attempt. Its colonial-type gridiron plan, historically the expression of indefinite extension, its abandonment of all the Baroque imagery which reached its final expression in Brasilia, its growth by feedback and flexibility – everything about it confirms its acceptance of Jane Jacobs' dictum that a city cannot be a work of art.* It also significantly abandons the struggle to

* In the conventional sense. But here is Jackson Pollock: 'When I am in my painting, I am not aware of what I am doing. It is only after a sort of "get

impose higher densities than are desired. Houses with gardens are unquestionably what most people want, and will need more than ever as the working week shortens and telecommunications make it more and more unnecessary to leave home; they are an anchor (if the gardens are large enough) holding people off the roads and the need for weekend cottages; and they keep in stock, used *pro tem.* for ornamental purposes, thousands of pocket paddocks where some kind of future food could if necessary be grown.

Practically, by a process of confluence, the whole of Great Britain south of the Highlands seems destined to become an urban region – it will certainly be a curious and varied region, far less monotonous than our present English world – perhaps rather more abundantly wooded, breaking continuously into park and garden and with everywhere a scattering of houses. Each district, I am inclined to think, will develop its own differences of type and style. As one travels through the urban region one will traverse open, breezy, 'horsey' suburbs, smart white gates and palings everywhere, good turf, a grand-stand shining pleasantly; gardening districts all set with gables and roses, holly hedges and emerald lawns; pleasant houses among heathery moorlands and golf-links, and river districts with gaily-painted boat-houses peeping from the osiers. Then presently a gathering of houses closer together and a promenade and a whiff of bands and dresses, and then, perhaps, a little island of agriculture, hops or strawberry gardens, fields of grey-plumed artichokes, white painted orchard, or brightly neat poultry farm. Through the varied country the new wide roads will run, here cutting through a crest and there running like some colossal aqueduct across a valley, swarming always with a multitudinous traffic of bright, swift (and not necessarily ugly) mechanism; and everywhere amidst the fields and trees linking wires will stretch from pole to pole. . . .

The same line of reasoning that leads to the expectation that the city will diffuse itself until it has taken up considerable areas and many of

---

acquainted" period that I see what I have been about. I have no fears about making changes, destroying the image, etcetera, because the painting has a life of its own. I try to let it come through.'

the characteristics, the greenness, the fresh air, of what is now country, leads us to suppose also that the country will take to itself many of the qualities of the city. The old antithesis will indeed cease, the boundary lines will altogether disappear: it will become, indeed, merely a question of more or less population.*

H. G. Wells' astonishing forecast of 1902 seems to be valid still.

But if this is the trend, then our sense of living in the organic world can only be sustained by illusion, and perhaps after land conservation this is the second of the techniques we will need to master. Fortunately the British school of landscapists have been illusionists for generations, often unconsciously. The motivation of the Picturesque was to create in a grey and windy island an illusion of the Golden Age. In Richard Wilson's English and Welsh landscapes, Perugino's delicate aspens and Poussin's monumental sycamores stand motionless, not a leaf stirring, against skies as luminous as those of the Campagna in September; and photographers will still wait weeks for that golden evening with long shadows, will neatly exclude the power-line and the parked car, in deference to the same dream. And it is all done in what are by continental standards diminutive spaces. William Kent's vistas at Chiswick double back on themselves like a 9-hole golf course, and his eyecatchers both there and at Rousham are scaled down to increase the illusion of distance. His Horse Guards too is absurdly tiny for the grand elements of which it is composed – and unfortunately seems so now in its Victorian setting. Opposite, St James's Park is perhaps the most fascinating example in Europe of how to make a magic world of its own out of a quarter mile strip between two main roads; and Hyde Park until lately was a limitless pastoral landscape, with sheep grazing in its clearings from which the towers of Westminster could be seen unbelievably far away, and to the west nothing but the sunset, so that one had the sense of all the western counties flooding in through that open door. In the same way you can still look outwards from the heart of Edinburgh and Bath and Oxford at illusory mountains or

* H.G. Wells, *Anticipations of the Reaction of Mechanical and Scientific Progress upon Human Life and Thought* (1902).

meadows or rich woodlands, only the map betraying the miles of suburbs beyond. In Pope's words:

> He gains all points who pleasingly confounds,
> Surprises, varies and conceals the bounds.

Spatial illusionism of this sort is one kind of magic. Another is the secret garden or enclosure that creates the illusion of with-drawal: the Cambridge court entered through its tiny mousehole, the privileged Inns of Court sequestered back of the noisiest streets in London, the walled open-air rooms of Sissinghurst, the walls of every town garden or glimpsed green patio concealing a million private paradises, the walled cities impenetrable by motor-cars, where echoes change their pitch as you pass through their dark gates, and at their heart the walled cathedral close with its green carpet.

Great trees and great walls: by a right use of these two we command the sense of mystery without which life in a crowded world would be intolerable.

Conversely and by contrast we have to foster in crowded countries the illusion of infinite space. Most British climbers know the story of the Swiss guide looking at the peak of Snowdon from the snowbound ridge of Crib Goch (an hour's walk) and doubting whether the climb could be completed before nightfall. One nuclear power station in those miniature Alps, one hydro-electric dam high on the hillside, and the whole illusion collapses. No doubt the planet still has more unbearable deserts, more snowy wastes, more barren meaningless ranges of mountains, more 'vast edges drear, and naked shingles' than suits our scared agoraphobic natures. But in the great tracts of Europe and Asia and America where we swarm those wildernesses seem infinitely far away, and the accessible wild places correspondingly precious. It seems that it is our actual knowledge of their illusory wildness that gives them their charm: better than the real thing. But the illusion is precarious and vulnerable to one false step, and to protect it against exploitation or merely ignorant forces will always be a hard fight.

This does not mean that we need cling to the literary, associative, sentimental haze through which the English landscape has been reviewed for two centuries. On the contrary, the parameters can be given their head here as elsewhere. Nan Fairbrother, the Jane Jacobs of landscape, has reminded us that the net of hedges and the myriad hedgerow trees that are now our 'heritage' were absolutely not wanted when they were introduced by John Evelyn and his followers in the seventeenth century: conservatives fought like tigers for the rolling English prairies across which you could ride so freely. Now we must face the fact that the trees are on the move again, because they are an economic burden on the farmland but an essential recolonisation of our denuded moorlands and mountainsides, where the first of the great forests of the future are already established. It follows that our descendants will sweep across the great cornlands for a sense of space, and vanish into the forest glens and cwms for a sense of mystery.

> Under a pine, when summer days were deep,
> We loved the most to lie in love or sleep:
> And when in long hexameters the West
> Rolled his grey surge, the forest for his lyre,
> It was the pines that sang us to our rest,
> Loud in the wind and fragrant in the fire,
> With legion voices swelling all night long,
> From Pelion to Provence, their storm of song.

Outcry from all preservationists! Roy Campbell, of all discredited poets! But our insatiable hardwoods, with their associated communities of plants and animals, are not going to fade away as meekly as that. Their almost miraculous powers of colonisation have been proved in our time on a thousand bomb sites, spoil heaps, industrial wastelands and neglected open spaces. We can confidently expect that along the slopes of every winding uncultivable lowland valley, beside every beck and burn and new reservoir, and along the flowery verges of every enticing country lane (if we have the sense to close it to cars), the English arcadia, the half accidental half contrived product of English illusionism, will go forth and multiply.*

* I owe this line of thought wholly to Nan Fairbrother's *New Lives New Landscapes* (1970).

To Conservation and Illusion we may add a third necessity if life is to be tolerable in a crowded world: the need for Identification. Of course the three are quite different in kind. Conservation is a goal, I would say *the* goal, and nobody nowadays would question it. Illusion is a technique, worth remembering because easily forgotten. Identification is a psychic need and as such hypothetical until proved by experiment and experience. It can be defined as our need to belong, our need for a place which having its own uniqueness reinforces ours. Experience seems to show that people feel this need at three levels: in their homes, in their local community, and at the symbolic centre of their nations. Let us look at each of them.

Property is now to a large extent abstract and impersonal; it does not tell you anything of a man's mind and spirit if you learn that he has sold his General Motors stock and bought International Business Machines. Even the more tangible goods are not so much possessed as consumed: they are acquired and disposed of, leaving behind no trace, neither taking the character of their owner nor imparting anything of themselves to him. And as for owning a plot of earth, it now means less and less. New roads are pushed through near by. Housing developments surround it. The view, the very air, is cut off. A man's home is no longer his castle when the total environment is altered unrecognisably.

What the individual requires, therefore, is not a plot of ground but *a place* – a context within which he can expand and become himself. A place in this sense cannot be bought; it must be shaped, usually over long periods of time, by the common efforts of men and women. It must be given scale and meaning by their love. And then it must be preserved.★

It is remarkable that in this passage August Heckscher as an American does not, as most English writers would, claim for the family hearth and home the primacy in conferring on people a sense of identity: he claims it for the community, a traditionally much more emotive word in the United States than it is in Europe, because it was the colonists' sole security in a hostile environment. And we all know from our own experience that the territorial

★ August Heckscher, *The Individual and the Mass* (1965).

imperative does not need a private patch of earth for its satisfaction. With the aid of a few pin-ups and sacred objects the schoolboy in his dormitory, the monk in his cell, the sailor in his hammock, the soldier in his foxhole, the student in his digs, the typist at her desk, will stake out their claims and fortify a minimal sense of security. A woman only needs to set out her night things in a hotel bedroom to feel at home. While no one with any experience of housing problems would wish to fall back on these examples as pretexts for inactivity, they do suggest a need for careful assessment of priorities. Thus Professor Mallows, attaching an academic precision to the word 'know', can write: 'We do not even know whether physical improvement (e.g. new housing) is a social good – there is evidence from contemporary Pakistan that people are healthier in shacks because they can afford more food.'*

For architects, and particularly for British architects with their compulsion to make Architecture out of housing – itself a creditable reaction from the Victorian failure in this field – the lesson is that this is the last thing that people want,† or anyhow the last word that they would use to express their wants. What they want is first shelter and services adequate for their needs, second a sense of security, and third the freedom to achieve a sense of identity, which is best done by making one's own unique mark in the world. In England no doubt this may mean primarily a garden, though it can mean other things as well, such as a crazy fence, a pop colour scheme, frilly nylon curtains or a backyard workshop. In rockier or more arid countries these latter items come first. The role of the architect in either case is to provide not a townscape but a framework, a platform on the ground or in the air, a network of services to which one can plug in. And his skill and subtlety will be to so order this pattern that when filled in (like the numbered dots in the child's puzzle) it crystallises into a life-enhancing environment. No doubt one of the reasons why so

* E.W.N. Mallows, *Physical Planning, a Social Process* (Johannesburg 1967).
† A survey conducted in 1969 found that 'good design' rated lowest of the qualities sought after in new housing.

many people prefer the feel of the back streets of old towns to the new public housing on the fringes is that the former, whatever the merits of their original 'architecture', have been through this process. Our task is to make deliberate and easy what in the past has been anarchic and against the grain of the planner's orderly mind – the creative tension between spontaneity and decency being in this field as in wider ones the essence of a successful society.

Of course this is not the whole truth. There are people to whom this sort of freedom could be an embarrassment, and who want nothing better than a handsome or conventional or fashionable exterior, behind which they may or may not choose to create a private world. Some people's central need is for a firm structure for which they do not have to feel responsible, or in which they can take pride by proxy. The truth is many-sided, and I have simply put the emphasis on its neglected side.

The words 'pride by proxy' bring us to the next level, the locality where we belong and feel we are, as they say, 'somebody'. Originally nothing more than a big plane tree or a bench in the sun for the men, and the village pump for the women, this is the centre of reassurance we dream of in war and exile, abandon in impatience or need or ambition, often to return, reoccupy and defend in old age. We can identify it in an unfamiliar country more by the tenacity of its users than by its architecture: it may even be ugly, will generally be shabby, will invariably be over-crowded. British planners call it the 'historic core', note its tiny extent in relation to the built-up area as a whole, mark it a Con-servation Area and hope for the best. Civic societies passionately defend its every cobblestone. The cynical view is that it is strictly a minority interest, mainly concentrated in elderly ladies of the professional class.

I doubt if this relaxed attitude will suffice much longer. Those elderly ladies have generally been right in the past, and what they defend here is more than bricks and mortar; it is the need for what Simone Weil called *l'Enracinement*, most deeply felt when we are deprived of it. In any case this particular good cause, in Britain at any rate, is moving out of the area of charity into the area of accepted public responsibility: it is acquiring its own operational lore. It is clear now that urban heart trouble is due to two causes: clogged circulation and decayed tissue. We know the cost of the double operation necessary, and we know it can be afforded. The historic core of York for example has within its medieval walls no less than $2\frac{1}{2}$ million square feet of industry and warehousing, much of it in what were the back gardens of handsome town houses. Yet so great will the benefit be of diverting traffic out of its narrow streets that it has been calculated that at a cost well within the city's means twenty-four acres could be cleared of industrial encroachment and restored to housing, and all the best old houses in the walled city be given sufficient support to safeguard their future. Public opinion polls seem to have established that this is not only possible but desired. Yet York is a notoriously hard case; most old English towns present fewer problems.

But then the United Kingdom, with its highly developed social conscience and nowadays almost spinsterish concern for its heritage, is almost the last country in the world where the sense of identity is likely to decay. It is in this respect so far ahead as almost to be irrelevant. The tower blocks that seem to us so inhuman are pretty toys beside the giant tenements of Moscow and Manhattan, and there are few sights more ominous than the brand-new housing super-slabs of Hong Kong and Singapore, where a hundred people have to manage on the land-space taken by one house at Harlow. No one should be deceived by the neat and smiling Chinese and their highly artificial economies into supposing that anything but a social disaster can sooner or later ensue from such living conditions.

This is not a guess. We have terrifying evidence already, for example in the Cornell Medical School study of Midtown Manhattan. In this mixed but largely prosperous residential district east of Park Avenue, where the average density is 600 persons per acre twenty per cent were so mentally incapacitated as to be indistinguishable from patients in mental hospitals, a further sixty per cent showed symptoms short of impairment, and only twenty per cent were free of the symptoms of mental disease.*

Confronted by such evidence our memory of the *boule* pitch in a Provençal village or the age-old banyan in an Indian one seems like a folk-memory of some lost Atlantis. How much longer, one wonders, can the human race cling to these symbolic patches of bare earth? Any day now there will be a better all-weather material made of plastic, or the site will be taken for a car-park. The oppression of irresistible numbers pursues us all over the world. Even the mountain-top is not immune.

> The big mountains sit still in the afternoon light,
>   Shadows in their lap;
> The bees roll round in the wild-thyme with delight.
>
> We sitting here among the cranberries
>   So still in the gap
> Of rock, distilling our memories,
>
> Are sinners! Strange! The bee that blunders
>   Against me goes off with a laugh.
> A squirrel cocks his head on the fence, and wonders
>
> What about sin? – For, it seems
>   The mountains have
> No shadow of us on their snowy forehead of dreams
>
> As they ought to have. They rise above us
>   Dreaming
> For ever. One even might think that they love us.
>
> *Little red cranberries cheek to cheek,*
> *Two great dragon-flies wrestling;*
> *You, with your forehead nestling*
> *Against me, and bright peak shining to peak –*
>
> There's a love-song for you! – Ah, if only
>   There were no teeming
> Swarms of mankind in the world, and we were less lonely!†

* Ian McHarg, *Design with Nature* (New York 1969).
† D. H. Lawrence, 'Sinners', from *Look We Have Come Through* (1917), reprinted by permission of Laurence Pollinger Ltd and the Estate of the late Mrs. Frieda Lawrence.

We may turn from these desperately-threatened unities and localities to the city centre, where numbers seem to matter less because they have always been its raw material. Here it is not our own mark we make or our own roots we cling to; we bask in collective pride; we go up to Town for a taste of reflected glory; we identify with the Nation:

> When million-footed Manhattan unpent descends
> to her pavements ...
> When Broadway is entirely given up to foot-passengers and
> foot-standers, when the mass is densest,
> When the façades of the houses are alive with people, when
> eyes gaze riveted, tens of thousands at a time ...
> I too rising, answering, descend to the pavements, merge
> with the crowd, and gaze with them,
> Superb-faced Manhattan!
> Comrade Americanos!*

This suits architects much better: a sea of faces is as good as a stretch of smooth water for reflecting great buildings. Hence the lost image of the *Stadtkrone*, the Acropolis, the Capitol, the Campus, where an ennobled human race is pictured, as in Raphael's *School of Athens*, strolling in free air, deep in thought and talk. In fact at least half this metropolitan crowd are probably cosmopolitan – elderly tourists, business visitors, families on package tours, foreign students in local universities, hippies living on air. Another quarter will be provincials, fans up for the Cup, girls looking for room-mates, schoolchildren doing the National Gallery and the legislature, village women on a coach outing. Of the 'native' quarter the majority will be government office workers or downtown employees of great private combines, commuters mostly from remote suburbs, to whom the city centre is as impersonal a workplace as a factory. Only very rarely, for a procession or a riot or a firework display, do the real locals emerge from their slum warrens or sky-flats. The city centre certainly doesn't belong to *them*.

The essence, in other words, is diversity – a meal of many

* Walt Whitman, *A Broadway Pageant* from *Leaves of Grass* (1855).

courses rather than one *cordon bleu* masterpiece. If, ignoring the many failures, we look over the succession of the most reputable new towns and cities of this century – Canberra, New Delhi, Chandigarh, Brasilia, Tapiola, Harlow, Vällingby, Islamabad, Cumbernauld – we shall probably decide that their lack of history and consequent lack of diversity is their worst handicap. It is as though Paris possessed only the Louvre–Arc de Triomphe axis, London possessed only its stucco terraces, Rome only the Sistine vistas and obelisks. Great spaces are no substitute: great spaces do not attract the great crowds they so need to justify their existence. Perversely, the crowds prefer window-shopping to admiring civic architecture, and it is the hideous Oxford Streets, the Grands Boulevards, the Chandni Chowks of this world that draw them.

> Everything's up to date in Kansas City:
> It's better than a magic lantern show!

If it is not generous space, not great architecture, not freedom from traffic that draws the crowds (and London's Piccadilly Circus seems to prove all three) what is it? We have to look harder at the successes and failures to find the answer. First, I would say, centrality – the feeling that one is at the hub of the wheel. This is outstandingly the quality of St Peter's Square in Rome and St Mark's in Venice, and it is almost independent of their architecture. As a space, St Peter's 'leaks' badly at its western entrance, but it feels what it is: the pilgrimage centre of the Catholic world. St Mark's is enclosed on three sides by indifferent architecture, but its spatial perfection and the buzz of talk as you enter it have made it, as Goethe called it, 'the drawing-room of Europe'. Right down the scale of grandeur from Siena to the humblest hill-village, the *piazze* of Italian towns have this infallible touch of centrality. In their own inferior way – and again independently of their architectural quality – Trafalgar Square and Rockefeller Plaza have centrality, whereas Paris and all the modern cities that have copied its vista-planning have no introvert central space, because the irextrovert shafts of space pierce and destroy the sense of enclosure.

146

This sense of enclosure is, no doubt, the second vital attribute. Ever since Camillo Sitte it has been repeatedly analysed and advocated, partly in delayed reaction from the cold, correct and draughty characteristics of Parisian *Beaux-Arts* planning. Indeed a retreat to the obscure and mysterious nooks and crannies associated in the literary imagination with the Middle Ages was a notable feature of the Romantic movement, and was popularised in the work of Edgar Allan Poe and John Martin long before it penetrated the mind of the architect. It is now too well-established in the conventional wisdom to need any recapitulation here. We may note in passing that the current British doctrine, that there should always be if anything too little space for people (as in the House of Commons), rather than too much (as in the House of Lords), is of some historical interest, since hitherto town builders have always gone for the opposite extreme, generally for reasons of prestige: there were never in the past enough people to furnish the great Baroque set-pieces. Possibly we tend to go too far in the new direction. Certainly we seldom nowadays exploit the marvellous sensation to be had in temperate climates by creating a great south-facing sun-warmed wall from which a cossetted crowd can look out upon a beautiful panorama: the Royal Crescent effect, or the Rue de Rivoli or Princes Street sensation.

But necessary though this sense of security and protection is to our comfort, we also need its opposite. For a city to be truly identifiable we need to stand on some high place and see and hear it as a whole. Rome at sundown from the Janiculum, Paris from the terrace at St Cloud, Edinburgh from Arthur's Seat, Athens from Lycabettos, Hong Kong from Victoria Peak: the list is familiar and can be long. Of all examples, perhaps the most striking is the most recent – the parapet-less elevated platform at the feet of the double skyscraper-pylon which marks the nodal point of Costa's immense neo-Baroque layout at Brasilia. This sun-soaked and windswept belvedere commanding all the horizons must be the most dramatic city-centre in the world. It is the *Stadtkrone* in its purest form, the Corbusian acropolis more effectively realised than the Master ever achieved in his own work – one of those 'brilliantly sterile images' for which Lewis Mumford found him so to blame. The sterility of Brasilia, for Mumford, lies in its lack of emotional resonance: a trumpet-call, perhaps, exciting but soon gone, compared with the unfathomable symphony of which the great city's full orchestra is capable.

For finally it is the intricacy of the blue and white planet which binds us to it by so many ties; and it is the architect's congenital blindness to this that has made him so suspect. One can call it congenital because while it was a notable trait of the 'modern' architect, it was equally notable in the Victorian, Regency, Georgian, Baroque and Renaissance architect. Ruskin and the Pre-Raphaelites believed that we were different in the Middle Ages, and Gilbert Scott, under their influence, would send the sculptor of his Gothic capitals and bosses out into the country lanes to collect hedgerow plants to copy. Yet all the while he and his contemporaries were perpetrating brutal assaults on the classical urban scene and there is no reason to think that the medieval or Byzantine builders, helping themselves among the Roman ruins to fluted shafts and Corinthian capitals, were any different. Each generation has believed itself uniquely possessed of truth and virtue.

No doubt this belief was the necessary head of steam that drove the engine that changed the world. This was all very well when the world's stock of natural capital was so infinitely greater than its exploiters could handle that it was immaterial that they burned the forests, turned cornlands into deserts, and used old temples and monasteries as quarries for building materials. It should be clear by now that we have somehow to do without this particular source of energy, and try another fuel.

London is a foretaste of the nomadic civilisation which is altering human nature so profoundly, and throws upon personal relations a greater stress than they have ever borne before. Under cosmopolitanism, if it comes, we shall receive no help from the earth. Trees and meadows and mountains will only be a spectacle, and the binding force that they once exercised on character must be entrusted to Love alone. May Love be equal to the task!

148

E.M.Forster, writing in 1908, correctly foretold the rootless culture that lay immediately ahead, but fell back, characteristically of that short idealistic interlude, on 'human relations' to hold us together. A couple of generations later it seems to have been conclusively proved that Love in his sense was not equal to that task, and we put forward the hypothesis – and it may be no better based than his – that Love in *our* sense may be the way in to the long process of reintegration.

The time has come to sum up this geosophy, to which we have come from so many directions of argument that their point of intersection may have seemed to lack definition.

First, it is more than one building thick, or one profession thick. The individual cell, the building, the group, the community, the city, the region, the land and water surface of the globe – in this nexus, which we had better not call a hierarchy if that implies degrees of importance, there is no break-point anywhere. Nor is there any break-point between the natural and the artificial environment. We live, we know, in a space-time continuum in which we are all both subjects and objects: we change it, and it changes us. In this continuum, construction equals destruction, and the only meaningful word is *change*. If it was once useful and meaningful to write of architecture as an isolable element in the ordering of change, it is so no longer. We can only write of the art of change.

We shall succeed in this art not by learning its theory but by understanding its material – or more simply not by Learning but by Understanding; and first, by understanding the world. In this world, in which we prospered and multiplied by exploitation, we shall only survive by striking a proper male/female balance between development and conservation. The changes we are going to make in the land surface, for example, will be blind and destructive unless we understand that in absolute significance its soil comes first, its structure second, its beauty third. It is easy to understand the importance of the soil, not nearly so easy in our present state of ecological knowledge to understand the complexities of the structure, the 'seamless web' of interdependence in which plants and animals and men are involved with one another. All too readily we rush on into considerations of beauty because these seem (erroneously) a sort of common language that demands less dedicated mental effort in those who speak it. In fact, in the landscape, it is pure frivolity unless the other two are right.

Let us take one example, the siting of a motorway. Transportation and the pattern of settlement have been interlocked since prehistory. Foot and horse produced an orderly universal constellation of farming (walking distance) and marketing (riding distance) settlements that survives in many parts of the undeveloped world. The stage-coach produced ribbon-development along main roads. The railway produced a necklace with a bead at each halt, unrestricted motoring again produced ribbon-development on a scale which required legislation to control it. The motorway produces a larger-scale necklace with a big bead at each interchange, and 150 m.p.h. trains will doubtless produce a jumbo one with cities at 100-mile intervals. So wherever we place a motorway or retain a railway, we face the likelihood of this. We also cut through what may be a millennial pattern of farm boundaries and local movement, carve regions up into new chunks, or create new thrusts of development and change if we take a new motorway into underused or misused territory. To provide fast transportation from A to B without a multifold analysis of the structure of the landscape through which it passes is therefore wholly destructive. This analysis will incidentally almost certainly lead us to fit our route into what Buchanan called the 'cracks' in the pattern, so as not to invade and destroy its living cells.

Buchanan defined his 'cracks' originally in an urban context, and exactly the same rules in fact apply whether we are dropping a new house into a village or a new shopping centre into a city. We must study the anatomy of the situation before its face. This is not just the conventional planner's assessment. It means understanding the forces that have shaped the physical environment, both natural and human, and imprinted its characteristic grain upon it, so that when we put our new object in their path it takes them, resists them, deflects them, just as a new ship takes the wind and water. Once we think in terms of this analogy, we see how easily and naturally practical considerations slip into aesthetic ones. Beauty takes third place simply because it is accustomed to following the other two.

It was the absolute inability of mid-Victorian architects to think in such terms, rather than their eccentric architecture, which undermined the viability of much of what they built. Occasionally of course this boorish unconcern for their neighbours would produce a popular monster like St Pancras Station or Tower Bridge. But for every one of these there were a score of Queen Anne's Mansions, Peabody Buildings and Charing Cross Bridges. And more serious, this unconcern became a habit that grew in unpleasantness with the growth in scale of building operations. With the modern movement it acquired a futurist panache that make it seem not a failing but a feather in one's cap. Against such odds the protest movement is bound to feel as exposed as a group of anti-apartheid demonstrators in a Rugby football crowd.

Ninety-nine times out of a hundred the architect should see himself as contributing a brushstroke or two to a collective work of art and science which changes with every contribution, rather than as sole author of an isolated statement in a static environment. The raw material of his design will be the perennial parameters of chapter 1, but his analysis of them and the resulting synthesis will be crude and lifeless unless informed by love, that is to say by an affectionate understanding of what human beings have tried to do there in the past, with whatever degrees of success and failure, of their present patterns of movement and rest within his field, and of the future life that will be lived there, in its own obstinate way, when he has come and gone. These patterns are not unpredictable, but they are everywhere complex, diversified by different customs and climates, and can be modified only with deliberation and cunning: you have to work with the grain, stroke the animal down-fur, set up no image that fails to take hold in the user's imagination.

It is with some sadness, when fighting one's way through the sudden gusts that sweep the concrete jungle through which the pedestrian reaches London's Hayward Gallery, that one catches sight of the one survivor (apart from the re-vamped Festival Hall) of the 1951 Exhibition – the one cheerful item in the solemn scene – a tree. That exhibition, the work of a group of youngish designers who would have been young but for the war, was inevitably and correctly cheap, frivolous, and expendable, and like the contemporary New Look it soon became a by-word for the rather tawdry and flimsy archness with which middle-class Kensington confronted the grim realities of post-war Britain: it was of course, by later standards, over-designed. And yet, pacing the grey terraces of the successor scene, one looks back, and forward, to a less indestructible environment with some nostalgia. We have been preached to long enough, we feel, and are in the mood for a subtler architecture, our servant not our master, that will leave us to do the talking – and the imagining.

Here, by contrast, is the architect's image of Killingworth township in north-east England:

> It is conceived as a 'castle town' with a hard edge to a parkland setting approached by a causeway across a lake 'as a drawbridge crosses a moat'. The social and commercial facilities are concentrated in the central area, or 'citadel', astride a north/south spine road. A collector road, or 'bailey', forms a loop around the central area and associated housing with housing access roads, or 'garths', radiating from it.

But the *Architect's Journal*★ goes on to criticise the lack of opportunity for expressing personal taste, the lack of 'community interaction' and conversely the lack of privacy. These criticisms are no doubt unbalanced if taken out of context. Architecturally, in the conventional sense of the word, this young town has been widely admired, and great pains have been taken to cope with its early social discontents. The question for us is whether these discontents would exist if the imagery were of the kind which immediately appealed to its Geordie inhabitants, and if the parameters of needs and wants had been more deeply studied, whatever the commonplace consequences.

Over and over again, facile solutions that miss out on some

★ *Architect's Journal* (19 November 1969).

parameter, and random images that have no collective force, have stultified the work of architects. Conversely, it is often the under-stated, modifiable environment, firm yet unobtrusive, that has survival value, because it uses human life and change as its surface expression. Without its tinsel and baubles the Christmas tree is dark and dull; without the tree, the decorations are aimless.

How far can the argument of impermanence and flexibility be stretched? It is fashionable to stretch it a long way, with the cult of Do-It-Yourself housing and the current preference for the aesthetic and social values of the shanty towns to those of the municipal flats on the plain below. This is a criticism of the rigidity and inhumanity of official mass housing rather than an intelligible aim. As soon as Do-It-Yourself reaches the level of the blue-collar worker in Anglo-Saxon countries we get Peacehaven and the sleazier parts of New Jersey and Long Island. It seems clear that it can only produce an acceptable environment in situations like the Scandinavian one where low densities are acceptable, carefully thought-out and flexible kits-of-parts are on the market, and firm public control exists over the ambient landscape.*

The strength of this point of view is in other words not as yet in its physical solutions, which are still immature, but in its ideology of gentle and tentative infiltration as opposed to massive inter-ference. It is the ideology of those who lie down in front of the bulldozer, of Patrick Geddes with his 'conservative surgery', of the poets from Pope to Baudelaire, and of philosophers as different as Nietzsche and Marcuse. Its validity seems somehow confirmed by the far greater pleasure we feel when we see groups of sound old buildings refurbished than replaced – a reflection, no doubt, of the natural process of cell renewal as opposed to the artificial destruction of the complete organism. Both in the landscape and in the city we rejoice to see the plant put on fresh leaves, hate to see it cut down.

* In his landscape appraisal of Washington, DC, Ian McHarg suggested a recommended 'palette' of building finishes and plant material, consistent with the geology and vegetation of the region. Questionable in a metropolitan context, this could certainly be made mandatory in low density development in areas of recognisable landscape character.

But we must face the fact that there are two powerful objections to this quietist line of thought. The first is that we do not live in this kind of society. In the western world the people who settle the scale of development and the fate of the physical world are not poets or even planners, but businessmen. It is what the market will bear, not what the environment can tolerate, that gets built, even in semi-socialist Britain. No municipality, however planning-oriented, can afford in the last resort to kill the goose that lays the golden eggs. Planning is a tough bargaining process in which values do get shifted around but within tacit limits that ensure that they are not on balance destroyed. It was when Ruskin, living admittedly in a more primitive capitalism, saw that what was wrong with the Victorian world was not its art but its social morality that he threw up aesthetics and wrote *Unto This Last*.

The true home question, to every capitalist and to every nation, is not, 'how many ploughs have you?' but, 'where are your furrows?' not – 'how quickly will this capital reproduce itself?' – but, 'what will it do during reproduction?' What substance will it furnish, good for life? what work construct, protective of life? if none, its own reproduction is useless – if worse than none, – (for capital may destroy life as well as support it), its own reproduction is worse than useless.*

Without diving too deeply into economics, most of us would accept the principle that a society should so order its affairs that people profit by acting in the public interest. To apply this principle, it must define its goals before it can adjust its incentives and disincentives, and it has been with goals that we have been concerned in these last two chapters. A city sprouting skyscrapers whose workers live in tin shacks may of course regard unrestricted commercial competition as its overriding goal, or it may have other goals and have made a hash of its incentives and disincentives. In the present climate of world opinion it is more likely to be the latter. Certainly we now know that societies with sensible aims that do not conflict with the survival of humanity can be much tougher with that goose than they had supposed. Paris has proved

* John Ruskin, *Unto This Last* (1860).

that you can hold down building heights and apply rigid rules of conservation in the central business district of a great capital without slowing down its boom, and in England Leslie Martin has shown that London could have redeveloped at the same densities without going high if it had bought more boldly and dealt in larger parcels of land. History will probably decide that the primitive planning of the mid-twentieth century failed in clarity of aim and moral force rather than financial power.

This is of course a moderate way of putting it, within the constraints of the society in which we live. We may soon be confronted with harder choices. Obviously growth as such, productivity as such, beg the essential question *of what*. If our kind of economy only works by leaving such questions to market forces whose criteria are saleability rather than need, we shall soon see that it does not have the capacity to save us, and we shall have to dismantle it. Whether we are able to do that – *not* to go to Mars, *not* to build SSTs, *not* to build an eight-lane highway but a four-lane one – who can tell? It may need the lifetime's savage devotion of another Marx to persuade the world that it is both practicable and necessary for the sophisticated countries to decelerate their own advance and deflate their material standard of living, so as to switch their spare capacity to the rescue of the rest of the world. 'There is no wealth but life.'

So profitability is no ultimate criterion, though it will bite hard in the early stages and we shall be wholly dependent on political action to get it deflected into beneficent channels. The second objection goes deeper. It is that all innovation has to be destructive, that we made our way in the world by burning the forests and slaughtering their inhabitants, that you can't make an omelette without breaking eggs.

Although as early as 1594 Clifford's Tower at York was preserved from destruction as a picturesque object, and ever since the eighteenth century ruins have been a source of pleasure, the preservation movement did not really get into its stride until William Morris founded the Society for the Protection of Ancient Buildings in 1877. It has been recognised ever since as an historical anomaly, not so much for its decent piety for the buildings of our ancestors as for its conviction, widely shared outside, that we could never hope to do as well. It was this which lent force to efforts to hold on even to second-rate old buildings; and it was this which had never been thought before. If it had, Sistine Rome, Nash's London, Napoleonic Paris, and Imperial Vienna could never have come into existence and the magical transformation of Manhattan which followed the introduction of the electric lift in the 1880s could never have occurred: New York would have remained a stodgily monotonous five-storey port for ever. These intensely human achievements were made possible by the traditional masculine egoism of the architect. Traditionally, great building operations have expressed national pride, individual wealth and the historical knowledge and bold imagination of a prestigious learned profession. In England predictably the architect/builder relationship still shows signs of the same snobbery (direct and inverted) as has long infected the relationship between 'pure' and 'applied' science. To justify and enhance their superior status, architects feel called upon to make impressive statements. Consequently to speak in such circles of conservation and modest infiltration can be to evoke a kind of castration-complex of the sort that afflicts an army when it has to hand in its arms.

There is no need to make a drama of this. By 'conservative surgery' Geddes meant exactly what he said: he did not abjure the use of the knife. And of course occasions do occur for the great statement, even possibly at the cost of something like the Sydney Opera House. It is simply that these occasions are infinitely rarer than architects are brought up to suppose. To return to Manhattan, the fact that all the paths and shrubberies of Mount-morris Park, Harlem's own central park, are carpeted with broken glass is of greater social relevance, and therefore of greater architectural significance, than all the bronze and glass of the gigantic mid-town offices and hotels or all the careful formal statements of the Lincoln Center. 'True civilisation,' said Baudelaire, 'does not lie in gas nor in steam nor in turntables. It lies in the reduction of the traces of original sin.' No one has ever seen this connection more agonisingly than Ruskin, as for example in his inaugural lecture as Slade Professor at Oxford:

You cannot have a landscape by Turner, without a country for him to paint; you cannot have a portrait by Titian, without a man to be portrayed. . . . The beginning of art is in getting our country clean, and our people beautiful.

For the man of action which the architect essentially is, there seems to be some scope here.

What will finally determine whether we are any good is not the profitability nor the pretentiousness of what we do. It is our submission to the parameters and the quality of our imagination. In both spheres we are still conspicuously immature. Writers are divided on whether a Theory of Architecture is nowadays possible or desirable. Consequently, and correctly, none is taught, and most students receive either explicitly or implicitly a perfunctory Bauhaus *Vorkurs*, a set of specialist subjects in no structural relationship with one another, a box of sample images passed surreptitiously around, and some nervous and superficial criticism of what they make of it all. Yet both in 'architecture' and in 'planning', via the parameters, a systematic approach to design is now practicable and teachable, and the elements of a rigorous theory in the scientific science – that is to say a tested hypothesis that if certain things are done or not done certain consequences will inevitably follow – can be identified. There is no reason at all why architects and planners should flounder in a miasma of subjective statement and counter-statement, where they can be picked off one by one by those whose book it suits to say that it's all a matter of taste. Much of the elementary wrongness of what goes on is not bad art but bad science.

It is the old story of a theory – in this case the primitive theory of functionalism – discredited through failure to accommodate unfamiliar or unrecognised phenomena. There can no longer be much doubt what these phenomena are – the acceleration in the change of use of buildings and of alterations to permit it, the import of alien elements often of a 'tasteless' or pop nature, the arrival of unexpected and often unsympathetic neighbours and, particularly on the level of city planning, the changes and complexities of movement patterns. This must find architectural expression in violent contrasts of scale, ambiguities, multiple use, and a tendency to give the idiosyncracies of the specific situation precedence over general principles. An ability to 'adjust to the circumstantial' (in Louis Kahn's phrase) must mean either a loose fit or an assembly easily taken to pieces and put together again. Either way, we have to expect a more casual, ironic, unfussy architecture than has been thought right since the middle ages.

That one can write without inconsistency of an architecture that is rigorous in one paragraph and casual in the next is an example of what is becoming a familiar paradox. For the more closely we investigate the phenomenal world, the more relative and contingent have to be the stories we tell about it. This in no sense relieves us of the obligation to investigate; it merely deprives us of any excuse for short-cut generalisations. What does emerge, inevitably, is a cast of mind exactly opposite to that of the Modern Movement, which was casual about its science and only rigorous about its aesthetics. In place of soft thinking and hard building, ours must be hard thinking and soft building.*

I look out from where I write across the roofs of London and I see the hard buildings of the 1920s rust and peel as the time of their demolition approaches. All over Westminster the monuments of Victorian grandeur are a problem, the cast iron and glazed brick tenements and offices are torn down, and what will survive are the little streets from the eighteenth century, Cowley Street and Queen Anne's Gate and Blomfield Terrace, incredibly

* Professor C. H. Waddington, discussing in *Beyond Appearance* (1970) the relationships between modern art and science, thus describes the cast of mind of contemporary science: '(a) The epistemological foundation. The observer does not wholly make what he observes, but his intrinsic character colours it. There is no strict objective-subjective dichotomy. The painter is *in* his painting, the scientist is *in* his science. (b) Chance plays a role amongst the fundamental mechanisms. (c) Everything "has a feeling for" (prehends) everything else; things have fuzzy edges. (d) On a more down-to-earth level; we live in surroundings and conditions that we ourselves make, not in any state of nature that we have to accept in its entirety.'

frail, bombed, patched, mended, converted, virtually rebuilt brick by brick like the cells of our own bodies. They and their contemporaries the enormous London plane trees seem to have a vegetable life quite different from the intellectual solutions of the architects. When we go among them with new buildings we had better tread lightly – not building their way, of course, with clay and wood, but inserting among them structures of extreme delicacy within which the same kind of endless amendment and renewal can continue. For we move into a situation, not merely a site. Thus Guy Brett, writing of the generation of sculptors that included Brancusi, Arp and Gabo:

> Their forms do not give the feeling of being dominated by their creator. ... They seem to be searching for balance, a balance that organisms have because they exist in a state of exchange, not domination, with their surroundings.*

In thinking of the urban fabric as an ecological system we have reached a parameter which is at the same time an image. It is a parameter in the sense that it is one of the 'constituent facts', as Giedion called them, which we have to allow to mould the environment. Its central characteristics are interdependence, random renewal and controlled but non-automatic movement. We do not yet of course have anything better than experimental techniques for marshalling these highly complex facts, and it is too soon to say which mathematical models will work or whether the biologists and ecologists will help us more. The first step is to be aware that these characteristics are *always* present, at all scales from the region down to the smallest group of dwellings, and that a designer who gets to work without first seeking them out is bound to fail, occasionally on a catastrophic scale.

But it is also an image, in the sense that structures and movement patterns have existed and acted upon one another for so many centuries that they have together created what we now call townscapes and landscapes rather than built and unbuilt land –

* *The Times* (24 January 1970).

collective images that have an identity in peoples' imaginations even if they have never been described or defined. Some landscapes, like the Mediterranean coasts or the North American wilderness or the English countryside, and some townscapes, like Paris and New York, exist much more vividly in this sense than others, and impose themselves on those who work in them. Others are more diffused or complex, and it is perhaps the lack of a vivid collective image of London which has weakened its planning authorities, so that despite their legislative powers they have had to assert themselves in an imaginative vacuum, where there was no consensus about the sort of place London was or is or should be. In such situations the collective image may have to be more localised; but the point is that it must always be a collective image that we identify and enter into, and not an arbitrary image that we wheel on to the scene.

Not always, to be exact, but ninety-nine times out of a hundred. For there remains the hundredth case, where the architect's imagination is original and powerful enough to impose his own concept, whatever the circumstances. Such originality is a great deal rarer than we suppose.

People praise originality, but do they know what they mean? As soon as we are born the world begins to work on us, and does so all our lives. What can we call our own, except energy, strength and will? If I could account for all I owe to predecessors and contemporaries, there would not be much left to my credit.*

Goethe lived in an age of privilege in which only a handful of people had the chance even to seem talented. And it was no doubt the universal spectacle of mediocrity masquerading as genius which set the iconoclasts and the functionalists off on their long search for an aesthetic Reformation. But perhaps as we move towards an age of almost universal leisure the buried kingdom of the imagination, which most people can only visit once or twice in a lifetime, or in dreams, or not at all, will become accessible to

* Goethe, *Conversations with Eckermann* (1836).

many more of us. Meanwhile, we may perhaps comfort ourselves in the words of my niece's poem:

> The country you would return to
> Is in you;
> It is no bolted Eden.
> In the quiet rooms of the past
> Colour, music, speech
> Will burn when you come to them.
> Like the heart of the other through a long love
> The patient clocks tick for your sudden return.*

* Lucy Beckett, *The Country you would return to* (1966).

Postscript

Politics and Beyond

One could leave it at that, as most writers on theory do, treating as another subject the problems of action. Unfortunately it no longer makes sense to do so, because we now know that theory and action interact, modifying one another. The medium, says McLuhan, *is* the message. But the trouble in this sphere of planning and building is that while on the level of ideology it is still just possible for expert and layman to communicate, on the level of technics it is becoming almost impossible. Take two English examples, the Wash project and the London motorway programme. Fully supported by restraint elsewhere, and fully exploited, the Wash project could exert a lunar attraction on the population tide of London and particularly on its footloose industries, and so enable residential densities and infrastructure costs in the metropolitan region to be lowered at last. In so doing, it would drastically reshape the armature of growth to which English official circles are at present attached, which roughly speaking is a thickening-up and ribbon-development of the existing network. It would have the same creative role as the building of the railways across the American West. But its side effects, let alone its direct costs, are so immense that the financial burden of evaluating the project in all its ramifications and the communications problem of making a full-scale evaluation comprehensible to public opinion, seem to be beyond the capacity of British governments at present.

The same problems of comprehension beset an inter-professional group which over the long evenings of six months attempted to form an opinion on the traffic plans for Greater London. Merely to read and understand the London Traffic Survey is no spare-time occupation for already overstrained professionals and would be out of the question for the man in the street. Yet how can any-body judge the solutions if they cannot judge the problem? And this is in any case a narrow and inadequate approach. For as all planners know, traffic and land-use are inextricably interlocked, and it is at least conceivable that it would cost less and produce a better pattern of life to disperse a great deal more of London employment and therefore housing over the southern half of England (including, incidentally, the Wash) – to release the pres-sure by attacking causes instead of, or at least as well as, effects. But no data is available to enable anybody to weigh this or other alternatives. Material is provided for a narrow-front judgement, and even this is overwhelming in its complexity. Material for a broad-front judgement, which is in general the only judgement worth making, seems again to be beyond our communication capacity.

These are two examples in one field of a universal and essentially political problem. Nowadays none of the great projects for which the world is taxed is submitted to the judgement of the taxpayer. Has anybody anywhere compared the cost-effectiveness of nuclear power-stations, monorails, world fairs, supersonic transport, inter-planetary travel and second-strike capability? And if they have, has anybody gone on to put these choices to our democracies as planks in intelligible political platforms? 'Let's do it' is the most that the voter has been offered. 'Let's put a man on the moon by 1970' – but no mention, in Kennedy's platform, of what this might imply in risks or sacrifices in other fields. No ordinary family, no community except a nation state, could afford to settle its spending priorities in this way.

The blockage in communication inexorably leads into a block-age in public acceptance even of the most patently desirable objectives. Presumably it is this, rather than traditional American antipathy to state action, which has inhibited progress in the two most vital sectors of US internal policy – conservation and state-aided housing. No country in the world has thought out the conservation of its natural resources more thoroughly than the United States, or presented its findings better. But the presentation has still not been vivid enough to persuade public opinion of the urgent necessity of state action to prevent development continuing to be almost wholly subjected to market forces, or of the truism that there is no other agency that could conceivably prevent it.

Now we all know how these things are supposed to be handled in democratic theory. Electorates are offered a choice of two or more election packages, each of which is supposed to be pervaded by a consistent style. These packages will contain items of a fairly straightforward nature, new ideas in indirect taxation, new social security benefits and so on. And they will also contain some of the more spectacular, but by no means all, of the party's technological projects. These will generally be treated as non-political, and will always be presented as isolated let's-do-it ideas. Costs, benefits, merits in relation to alternative projects, will never be set out in a way which makes judgement possible. The electorate then selects its package, all or nothing, and in so doing, and primarily, it selects its administration. It is accepted doctrine that once elected, the new administration are representatives, not delegates. They claim, and are allowed, authority to drop some projects and take up others, and although it is common for the opposition to demand a referendum when obviously unpopular projects are taken up, it is most uncommon for this demand to be acceded to.

No part of the theory, but an indispensable part of the practice, are the officials by whom all the technological projects are mediated. Their non-recognition is denoted by the absence of any symbolic provision for them from l'Enfant's plan for Washington: it was assumed that they would be tucked away in the Capitol in exactly the same way as Louis XIV's functionaries in a wing of Versailles. Yet it is through these 'servants', at all levels of government, that all our projects are introduced into programmes, defended, lived with and brought to completion.

The politician's task is to 'buy', and then publicly endorse, whichever projects, new or current, seem to him consistent with his party's political philosophy – to select from a bundle of bright ideas those which he believes he can combine into an intelligible and appealing package. As decision-maker, he of all people must understand the rationale of each one, and it is consequently necessary for the experts to present each in cost/benefit form so that fully-informed choices can be made. It is equally necessary for the decision-maker to be capable of reading the documents.

The 'electorate' is too generalised a term for the mass audience to whom the resultant appeal is directed. Really it divides on every issue into two clearly distinguishable groups, the informed and concerned, and the uninformed and unconcerned. There may be a minor amount of cross-movement between the two according to the issue under discussion, but on the whole the concerned are inclined to be concerned about everything, the unconcerned about nothing that does not affect their personal lives. A recent report commissioned by the British government on public participation in planning recognises the existence of these two groups, and assumes that the former will already be organised into civic societies and the like, while for the latter, whom it expects to be disorganised and alienated, it recommends missionary activity by officially appointed Community Development Officers.* This perhaps over-simplifies the pattern, since there are joiners and non-joiners in both groups, and the unconcerned majority is by no means the dim-wit *lumpen-proletariat* it is often mistaken for by superior persons. It has recently been reinforced by significant numbers of intellectual drop-outs particularly of the student generation. Similarly, the concerned minority has no mono-poly of virtue: many of them are busy-bodies blissfully out of touch with the way the world is going. But of the reality of the two groups in all modern societies there can be no doubt.

* *Public Participation in Planning* (The Skeffington Report) (1969).

And so we have this apparently universal pattern of the Four Estates:

The Experts
The Decision-Makers
The Participators
The Don't-Knows

Each has its characteristic expression, the first in the professional institutions, the second on the boards of corporations or the committees of government, the third in the voluntary societies and charities, the fourth in the public opinion polls. At public enquiries a confrontation occurs between all four, with the Experts defending or attacking the project in their professional roles, the Participators as its amateur critics, the Don't Knows guarding their own territory and the Decision-Makers making their decision at the end of the day.

Accepting the existence of the Four Estates, because they are there, what can one expect of them? Some people would say that their first duty, presumably the politician's first duty, is to put ends before means and secure a consensus upon the *goals* of society. This would be a traditional American view in contrast to the English tradition that if you join a club or a country you instinctively know and share its basic moralities. Marxists feel differently again: that there never can be a consensus and that politics is a football-match with a goal at each end. The issue is to some extent a semantic one dependent on the line, so hard to draw, between ends and means. For on the four main goals of modern societies there is in fact an international and increasing if not yet worldwide consensus: upon peace, population control, aid to the Third World and the conservation of resources. Of these only aid could be said to be 'political' in the traditional sense, with the middle classes tending to take a more liberal view of it than the workers. Below this level it is arguable that the stuff of political argument is all in the field of means, not ends.

All the same, narrowing the field down to that of this book, there are moments when for example a great city could be helped, as recently with Los Angeles, to stand back and ask itself what sort of place it wants to be, with the consequences of each alternative set forth as dispassionately as possible. This kind of objectivity, in contrast to advocacy planning, is part of, and brings one to, the role of the First Estate, the experts.

It can be divided into three: survey, plan and presentation. First, and in default of guidance from on high (and this will seldom be forthcoming because nobody except the experts can know what is possible) it should be his pride as a professional, rather than a technician, to write his own brief in the light of his own judgement about society's needs and wants. He is an ideas man – neither master nor servant – and society absolutely depends upon him to play to the full that subtle part. Second, he is a man who deals in alternatives, not in imperatives: it is his duty to look at them all as coolly and systematically as his technology allows, and he now has an armoury of computers to help in the task of evaluation. The *trahison des clercs* to which he will always be liable is the temptation to skip this and to use his arts of persuasion to sell an untested solution that has beguiled him. Architects are particularly vulnerable here, since it is traditional with them to choose a solution without ever revealing the alternatives or the rationale of the choice, in case the client gets out of hand and chooses differently. Third is this last process, not so much of persuasion as of elucidation. The expert has to translate the project from the esoteric and abstract language of technology in which it was born and developed, into the demotic language of human values in which it can be discussed. And in this language he has to give without bias the whole of the criteria by which a right and responsible choice can be made.

One only has to set out these three stages to realise how rare it is for any object to be conceived, evaluated or implemented in this way. For this the experts and the decision-makers must share the blame.

This Second Estate, the decision-makers, now has at call (though only in the highest echelons does it know it) a methodology just as elaborate and esoteric as the experts'. Books have been written about it* that like most textbooks make it seem even stiffer than it is. From the start the decision-maker has to contend with that clever and characteristic expert's technique of pushing a preferred project carefully wrapped up in what appear to be objective criteria, while at the same time neatly palming off all responsibility for its acceptance and implementation. Not surprisingly, the best training he could hope to have in following the mental processes of the expert is the general (not the specialist) part of the expert's own education. This applies particularly to the schools of architecture, because the systematic decision-making that is learnt, or should be learnt, in a design studio is very closely related, both in its intuitive and rational aspects, to that which goes on, or should go on, in the world of what used to be called politics. For politics, as we are nowadays often told, is fast ceasing to be an amateur and out-of-hours occupation, and coming closer every day to professional management. An average RIBA Council agenda is 40,000 words long – half the length of this book – and the decision-makers who have to digest all this come invariably from the group which has least leisure in which to do it. One may safely generalise that at all levels their main need is a sense of proportion, and their main lack a sufficiency of time in which to apply it.

The Third Estate, the participators, does not have a good public image. The masochistic devotion with which they set out into the foggy winter night for some underlit and underheated parish hall, when the rest of the world is cosily ensconced with the telly, is predictably an irritant to their slightly guilty fellow-citizens. So are their assumptions of disinterested virtue and hints of inside knowledge. For it is suspected, and often rightly, that they are really pressure groups in sheep's clothing, and that those evening man-hours earn them no right whatever of consultation by the decision-makers as though they were in any sense representative of public opinion. It is easy to go on from this to by-passing them when they become tiresome, which they habitually do, and appealing over their heads to the ignorant Fourth Estate. But to do this

* For example, Jeremy Bray, *Decision in Government* (1969).

is to commit a fatal error, because the only public opinion that is usable is the opinion of those who are interested in the question, whereas the opinion of those who have No Opinion is obviously not an opinion at all: it is a guess. Of course decision-makers, among their many value-judgements, have to judge the objectivity of participators' opinions and in most cases interpret a spectrum rather than search for unanimity. But to go outside the participators and count the heads of the Don't-Knows, which is the only safe way of electing a government, is generally the worst way of judging the merits of an idea.

And so we come to this Fourth Estate, with its two dissociated elements, the standing army of the indifferent and the fashionable club of the wilfully uninvolved. Seen from here, the other three Estates are a smug, an anti-life, even a sinister conspiracy. Seen from within that establishment, the Fourth Estate is a rabble which one can patronisingly expect to see diminish in numbers with the growth of education and leisure. Of these two viewpoints, the second obviously will not do, since the drop-out leaders are both highly educated and wholly leisured. The first is a rough version of the truth, since the first three Estates are in effect a mutually sustaining closed circle in which untruths can establish themselves impregnably. Such for example could be the amenity-society dream of a rural and urbane England, or the American Way of Life which writers and hippie leaders like Tom Wolfe and Ken Kesey have seen as a collective fantasy, in which most people 'are involved, trapped, in games they aren't even aware of'.* We would be wise, instead of writing off the Don't-Knows, to see them as the indispensable critics of all our assumptions, and the guardians, some conscious some unconscious, of values which are no less real for being undefinable – or anyhow undefinable in the kind of language in which this book is written.

Architects need to clear their minds of conflicting loyalties, as they go to work in this complex environment. They will no doubt recognise the Fourth Estate as the source of most of their

* Tom Wolfe, quoted by Tony Tanner in 'Edge City', *London Magazine* (December 1969).

images, and the other three as the source of most of their parameters. But they themselves cannot go wild. They belong among the experts, on whom the world absolutely depends if it is not to vaporise, poison itself or starve. Yet they must never allow themselves to be taken over or walled in by any governing class, because they also belong among the Don't-Knows by the mere fact that to some questions their only answer can be: 'I don't know; I feel.' Architecture has never been a criticism of society and never could be. Its role has always been, and still is, a role of reconciliation and reassurance.

A Note on Books

'Some people say that life is the thing, but I prefer reading', said that wicked old aphorist whom I quoted at the beginning. The message of this book has been that he was precisely wrong, that what matters is not knowledge, but understanding. Every experience, bitter or other, is grist to that mill, every argument, accident, football match, country walk, movie, ballet, love affair or disastrous holiday – and every book, whether or not it is about architecture. So strictly in that context, since one book, like it or not, leads to another, some guidance here may help some people.

Nobody should start modifying the physical world without having studied the succession of English naturalist/mystics who have tried to comprehend it – for example Gilbert White of Selborne, the young Wordsworth, Richard Jefferies, and in our day Jacquetta Hawkes (*A Land*, 1951). Closely allied to them in spirit are the men of synoptic vision, and first John Ruskin, to whose range of thought Kenneth Clark's paperback* *Ruskin Today* (1964) is the best introduction. Patrick Geddes' *Cities in Evolution* (1915) (P), and Lethaby's *Architecture* (1922) will lead in to Lewis Mumford's great *Technics and Civilisation* (1934) and *The City in History* (1961), both of which contain immense bibliographies. Still out in this area of the total environment we have Sir George Stapledon's pioneering and robust *The Land, Now and Tomorrow* (1936), then David Lilienthal's *TVA* (P, now out of print). Modern descendants, more handsome as books but darker

* The letter P after a title hereafter indicates that a paperback version is available at the time of writing.

in their emotional tone, are C. A. Doxiadis' monumental *Ekistics* (1968), and Ian McHarg's *Design with Nature* (1969). With these I would couple Alec Clifton-Taylor's delightful survey of our native vernacular *The Pattern of English Building* (1962) and Nan Fairbrother's refreshing *New Lives New Landscapes* (1970).

Parallel with this development in comprehensive thought, touching it at times, but reaching back beyond the Renaissance from which such thought derives, is the story of what used to be called Fine Art. Among innumerable guides to this is, of course, Kenneth Clark's very personal *Civilisation* (1969), and for detail the excellent Pelican *History of Art* series, especially the Summerson volume on British architecture 1530–1830 and the Hitchcock volume on the nineteenth and twentieth centuries. Among general histories of architecture, which come in all shapes and sizes, I would still give the palm to Nikolaus Pevsner's *History of European Architecture* (1948) (P), and among general books on aesthetics to Gombrich's *Art and Illusion* (1961), an excellent guide to modern sensibility, as is Geoffrey Scott's *The Architecture of Humanism* (1914) (P), to that of our grandparents.

And so we reach the modern movement, if one may still so describe it. For its antecedents and origins three books are outstanding: Peter Collins' *Changing Ideals in Modern Architecture, 1750–1950* (1965) (P), Pevsner's *Sources of Modern Architecture and Design* (1968) (P), and Reyner Banham's *Theory and Design in the First Machine Age* (1960) (P). Shorter general essays on modern architecture are Banham's own *Guide to Modern Architecture* (1962), J. M. Richards' *Introduction to Modern Architecture* (1940) (P), and Vincent Scully's lecture *Modern Architecture* (1962). Perhaps the soundest larger-scale survey is Joedicke's *History of Modern Architecture* (1959)

Then there is the work of the modern pioneers themselves. Le Corbusier's two masterpieces *Vers une Architecture* and *Urbanisme* (in the Etchells translations) are indispensable, as is the omnibus 1967 one-volume *Complete Works 1910–1965*, and there is a useful Frank Lloyd Wright anthology *On Architecture* (1941) (P). But the great FLW *Autobiography* (1943) is better reading. L. Moholy-

Nagy's *The New Vision* (1939) puts the essence of Bauhaus modernism more vividly than does Gropius in his *The Scope of Total Architecture* (1956). Hitchcock's and Johnson's *The International Style* (1931) is an equally good but less original period piece. Peter Blake's *The Master Builders* (1960) has useful short summaries of the careers of Wright, Le Corbusier, Gropius and Mies.

Dennis Sharp for the Architectural Association has compiled a comprehensive bibliography *Sources of Modern Architecture* (1967) whose criteria of inclusion and exclusion will themselves be of historical interest before long. All in all one can say that the canon of modernism is now very well documented. The same cannot be said of the classical authorities on architecture, so much of whose thought is still relevant. There is a paperback Vitruvius, but we badly need an anthology of the heavy leather-bound succession that stretches through the nineteenth century from Reynolds and Durand, to supplement the illuminating fragments dug out by Banham and Collins (*op. cit.*).

Finally, coming out on our side of the modern movement, I think the intuitions of Robert Venturi in *Complexity and Contradiction in Architecture* (1966), of Jane Jacobs in *Death and Life of Great American Cities* (1961) and of Christopher Alexander in *Notes on the Synthesis of Form* (1964) are important. Characteristic of our generation, but harder to digest and therefore to judge, are C. Norberg-Schulz's *Intentions in Architecture* (1963) and the group of essays collected by Charles Jencks and George Baird under the title *Meaning in Architecture* (1970).

The student who has read all these books will know his place in history all right, and will be equipped to add to their number. What he will also know is how little was known by those who made the greatest advances.

Index

Abercrombie, Sir Patrick, 77
Academies, contempt for, 42
Adelaide, 61
Adshead, S. D., 75
Arendt, Hannah, 108
Alberti, Leone Battista, 16, 20, 25, 62
Alexander, Christopher, 85, 87–8, 173
Amateurs overruling professionals, 103
American Scene, The, 71 n.
Amsterdam, 59
Angkor, 16, 90
Animals, relationship changed to, 117
Anti-change, 130–1
Anticipations of the Reaction of Mechanical and Scientific Progress upon Human Life and Thought, 137
Architect, 130; aloof aesthete, 120; from colleagues, gulfs separating, 127; human compulsions of, 13; -planners, wartime, 77; prestige no protection for, 131; superior virtue sensation, 18; to synthesise needs and wants, 4; traditional masculine egotism, 156; unpopular, 110–13
Architect's Journal, 152
Architectural Association Quarterly, 113
Architectural Forum, 83 n.
Architectural Principles in the Age of Humanism, 22 n.
Architectural Review, 35, 51 n., 74 n., 90 n.
Architecture from geo-physics, 5; geometric mechanical, 19; 'good manners' in, 6–7; of cathedrals, 16–17; parents of, 109; properly dressed, 40; questioned, Theory of, 157;

Renaissance emotions in, 19; rigorous yet casual, 158; six themes in modernist, 28; switch to diagrammatic, 33; systematic approach practicable, 157; thirteenth-century, 17
Aristippus, 23
Arp, Jean, 159
Athens, 4, 21, 147
Australia, 133

Bacon, Edmund, 23 n.
Baird, George, 173
Bangkok, 67
Banham, Reyner, ix, 27 n., 172–3
Barlow, W. H., 40
Baroque aesthetic, collapse of, 110
Barcelona, 31
Barr, Alfred Hamilton, 49
Bath, 24, 137
Baudelaire, Charles, 20, 153, 156
Bauhaus, 45–6, 50, 114, 119, 129, 157, 173
Beckett, Lucy, 161 n.
Beerbohm, Max, 26
Behrens, Peter, 33
Belle Epoque, 83
Bellow, Saul, 118
Berg, Max, 14
Berlage, H. P., 33, 45
Berlin, Sir Isaiah, 3
Betjeman, Sir John, 112
Bewick, Thomas, 104
Birmingham, 66, 123
Blake, Peter, 42, 173
Blake, William, 124
Bogardus, James, 40